Life's A Journey, Who Am I?

A MEMOIR

Stefanie Foster Freeman

Copyright © 2021 by Stefanie Foster Freeman

All rights reserved. No part of this publication may be reproduced, distributed, or transmitted in any form or by any means, including photocopying, recording, or other electronic or mechanical methods, without the prior written permission of the author, except in the case of brief quotations embodied in critical reviews and certain other noncommercial uses permitted by copyright law.

For permission requests, write to the author at:
stef@steffreeman.com

Life's A Journey, Who Am I? / Stefanie Foster Freeman — 1st ed.

Paperback: 978-1-7377683-0-2
Hardcover: 978-1-7377683-1-9

Dedication

I dedicate this book to Bob and Aud, my amazing parents. I am beyond grateful that our souls chose each other. You both taught me so much. Unconditional love, compassion, kindness, generosity, and the love of family. Thank you for loving my kids and instilling your values in them.

I wish you were here to see how hard I've worked to heal myself and start a business to help others heal. I wish I knew then what I know now, so I could have used all of these resources to help you both heal.

I wish we could chat one more time to get some questions answered, but I feel your presence around me at all times and you have in fact answered many questions. I love you both always and forever.

> *"If heaven weren't so far away,*
> *I'd pack up the kids and go for the day."*
>
> JUSTIN MOORE

I want to inspire people. I want someone to look at me and say, "Because of you I didn't give up."

Acknowledgements

I am so thankful to have such an amazing tribe of people that support me no matter the idea I have. They trust and believe in me. It certainly took a tribe for me to move through my healing journey and write book number two.

I must thank my parents. Although they were gone much too soon, their love and support has never been felt more than right now. I'm certain that the way they navigated their health conditions has set me on a path of not only healing, but of helping others heal. I feel their presence every day. Mom, I'm giving you total credit for the writing of this book. Dad, your messages come through to me loud and clear of how proud you are of me and that you believe I can do anything I set my mind to, and it means the world to me. I love so much the love you had for each other and all the valuable lessons you taught your family while you were earthside and beyond.

To my kids, you always support me no matter what I ask of you. Trying essential oils, using the Healy, and watching my storytelling pieces. I appreciate it so much. Kyle to see you as a dad to Rose makes my heart sing. Kris, you're a good dad to Hailey and Konner. Samantha, you are a strong, incredible woman, always up for a challenge and working so hard to create the wonderful life you have. Alana, you certainly found your calling when you became a mom to Aspen. I love the sisterly bond that you both have. It truly makes me happy. You make this world a better place.

Chris, I can come to you with any crazy idea and you always have the same response, "You've got this, Steffi." You are my chef, my tech guy, although I'm getting better at that, and my better half.

BJ, my bestie. I have no idea where I would be without your unwavering friendship. You are my inspiration. When you're proud of me that makes me happy. You are my unbiological sister.

Heather, it seems like we have been friends forever. Our weekly breakfast dates to solve the world's problems I love so much. To know that you are there for me no matter what and I for you is the most comforting feeling.

Janine, I would not be on this journey if not for your knowledge and friendship. Thank you for listening to all of my self-diagnosis and teaching me. We certainly laugh a lot and that's good for the soul.

Brenda, my mentor and friend. You have shown me in such a short time that my story is powerful and I must share it with the world. Your kindness, compassion, and intuitiveness have helped me grow as an author and storyteller.

Stu, I know some of what I am learning is helping you. If I could erase your pain, I would. You're a great bro!

CHAPTER 1

LIFE'S A JOURNEY, WHO AM I?

This book has been in the making for years. A few months after publishing *Life's A Journey, Are You Packed?: Living and Thriving with Juvenile Rheumatoid Arthritis* my health journey zigged and zagged and I knew I had to write another book. I found that I was getting even more clarity in ways to keep my inflammation level down and continue feeling great! I would think about it, talk about it, mention it to my husband and my functional medicine doctor, and put it on my to-do list. Somehow, I just never got around to it. Until now.

After the jarring events of the past two years, I knew the time was now. The universe wasn't giving me subtle hints, it was giving me a universal two-by-four over the head.

My hope is that some of what I have gone through will help you. We are never alone in our journey. We have our spirit guides, angels, and each other to walk this path.

My intention was always to start my second book exactly where my first one ended. I just wasn't exactly sure what that would look like or when the right time would be. I certainly contemplated the writing of this book for a few years. It wasn't until an event in my life happened in the fall of 2020 that I said to myself, "Stef, the time is now." Welcome to *Life's A Journey, Who Am I?*

My book *Life's A Journey, Are You Packed?* ended with me finding an amazing functional medicine doctor and doing a DNA test on 23andme. She ran my results through a medical algorithm to see what my genetic predisposition was and helped me get on a path to turn that around. This genetic testing would take me on quite an unexpected journey. I know now more than ever my autoimmune disease and my ancestry journey is for a very important reason: to help people. I am an open book in *Life's A Journey, Who Am I?* My intention is when we share ourselves with others, we really do find common ground. It then makes us realize we are not alone, we are together on this journey of life to support and hold each other up. Feeling less alone is the key component for me to healing.

> *"We read to know we are not alone."*
>
> C.S. LEWIS

Life's A Journey, Are You Packed? is about my holistic healing journey. It takes you all the way back to when I had my first symptom at age 3, until my diagnosis at age 11 and other diagnoses in my adult life. The old saying "Hindsight is 20/20" sure is the truth. The understanding of autoimmune diseases from a holistic approach allowed me to look back on my health over the previous 50 years and get a much better understanding as to why I felt the way I did, why I had the symptoms I had, why I always got sick, why my weight fluctuated, why I had trouble getting pregnant, and why energy was always so elusive. All of it! Did I get better overnight? Am I completely healed now? Heck no, not yet. Hence the title of both books so far, *Life's A Journey...*

Being armed with all of this information made it so much easier to zig and zag in my health journey. Dietary changes, supplement changes, exercise changes, all of it. I was so fortunate to have connected with my functional medicine doctor. She is not only my doctor, but a dear friend who allowed me to tag along to a functional medicine convention. She is open to my theories on why certain things are bothering me; sometimes I'm even right. Autoimmune disorders are such a heavy subject, but we laugh through it. Your mindset is everything and my mom always taught me, it can always be worse. She was right. These pesky autoimmune diseases do not define me. They are not me. So I spend my time slowly but surely kicking them out of my body. I have enough wonderful friends, these are not my friends; so they can leave.

I hope you enjoy taking this next journey with me. Full of twists and turns, eczema and hot flashes, new diagnoses, and a family secret. Buckle up. Are you ready for the ride?

The two most important days in your life are the day you are born and the day you find out why.

MARK TWAIN

CHAPTER 2

HEALING WITH DR. LEX

After seeing my parents navigate their health through conventional medicine, I knew there was another path for me. I believe in the combination of Western and Eastern medicine. In 2016, I was introduced to Dr. Janine Lex, a functional medicine doctor, chiropractor, and acupuncturist. It was a one-stop shop for me. Our journey together began with blood work, a treatment plan, and genetic testing.

I listened to everything she told me to do, and slowly but surely I started to feel even better, until I didn't. That is the journey of autoimmune diseases. In the spring of 2017, I began to have VERY itchy legs. I would describe them to my husband Chris as feeling itchy from the inside. I would spend half the night scratching my legs until they had bruises or bled. There was no rash, but they were so itchy. I also would tell Chris that I'm always chilly, chilly on the inside, and he would laugh and say that isn't a thing. In fact it was!

After a few months, I decided that I should mention this to Dr. Lex. What I love most about Dr. Lex is her calm demeanor. She always listens and processes. Many times I would come in with a symptom and self-diagnosis. Sometimes she would agree, other times she would just laugh. After I discussed these new symptoms, she sent me to the lab for some blood work. The next day her office manager called me and said, "Dr. Lex wants to see you this afternoon to discuss your blood work results."

THIS AFTERNOON? I immediately thought, *Oh no, what's wrong?* I did what I tell my kids never to do: I googled itchy legs on WebMD. Oy vey!!

I arrived at her office 15 minutes early in a ball of nerves. As I walked into her office, she invited me to sit down. She said that I looked stressed. I told her that I'd been googling. She laughed and told me to take a deep breath and relax. She then delivered the news. "Has any doctor ever told you that you have Hashimoto's?" I looked at her. That's it? That's what I have? Oh I've got this! No doctor had ever mentioned it to me. Dr. Lex thought I possibly had it without being diagnosed for about 20 years, which explained the exhaustion and difficulty losing weight. Hashimoto's thyroiditis is the most common form of thyroiditis in America. It is an inflammation of the thyroid gland and an autoimmune condition.

We came up with a plan. My eating would continue as is, no gluten, no dairy, no refined sugar, no pre-packaged foods. She added a few supplements including, selenium. As soon as I started taking selenium, the itching in my legs, from the inside, went away. The other thing that helps with Hashimoto's is iodine. I was very iodine deficient. She gave me a roll-on bottle of iodine to roll on my stomach in a 2-inch by 2-inch square. When it disappeared, I would repeat. It didn't take very long for the iodine to disappear. After a few weeks, my upper body suddenly became very itchy. I thought we had this itching stuff figured out. One night shortly after noticing the new itchiness, I woke up in the middle of the night and sat straight up. It came to me. My mom went into anaphylactic shock during an upper GI procedure from the iodine in the contrast dye they had injected into her! Could I have the same issue? I discontinued the iodine and the itching went away. Another time as Dr. Lex was tweaking my supplements for my thyroid she gave me a new one. I began taking it as instructed and became itchy. I flipped over the bottle and there was the tiniest bit of iodine in the supplement. This iodine allergy was a real issue.

Dr. Lex and I continued to work together. I learned so much from her. We have done many seminars on Young Living essential oils, non-toxic living, and Healy. I was so honored when she invited me to go with her to the 2018 Institute for Functional medicine Conference in Hollywood, FL. I soaked in so much information from every session. The first evening at the dinner, I met and was able to speak with Dr. Mark Hyman. Dr. Hyman leads a health revolution, revolving around using food as medicine to support longevity, mental clarity, happiness, and a lot more. He is a practicing family physician and advocate in the field of functional medicine. In other words, he is my go-to for education in this realm. His podcast *The Doctor's Farmacy* is my favorite podcast. He is a wealth of knowledge, as well as his guests.

I encourage everyone on a health journey to do your research and check out all of your options to see what resonates with you. Functional medicine and its healing modalities speak to me.

When I was at the Arthritis Foundation Conference for Juvenile Idiopathic Arthritis (formerly Juvenile Rheumatoid Arthritis: JRA), a few years ago, all of the attendees and volunteers were encouraged to make a necklace with a colored plastic bead or beads corresponding with their diagnosis. I had a purple bead for JRA/JIA. I was working at the sign-in table where I directed speakers to the proper rooms for their talks. I had many eye-opening conversations. I will share them here. I am not a doctor nor am I making any claims as to what you should do. I'm just someone navigating her own journey and getting as much information as possible to make informed decisions for my own health. As I sat at the table, a rheumatologist came up to ask me which room he would be speaking in. He noticed my necklace and said, "Oh, I see you have JIA, clearly you are not a child any more." Why do you say that? Then we both laughed. He asked which biologic drugs I was on and I told him that I don't take any medication, I control it through diet, exercise, and functional medicine. His whole face changed and he looked at me like I was going to be reprimanded. And I was correct. He said, "Please don't tell that to anyone because they will think they can do it and they can't." I asked him to consider the possibility that he could suggest his patients make lifestyle changes and to see if it had any effect. He said, "I suppose, but I didn't learn much about nutrition in medical school." It was left at that. He turned and huffed away. I sat there in absolute disbelief. How sad that lifestyle changes and reducing inflammation weren't standard information for everyone.

I spoke with many other people at the conference who were on biologic drugs and other medications that developed secondary issues or cancer. My heart really hurts for all of these people. Eating healthy and moving your body is never a bad thing. I don't understand why it is not the first go-to treatment. Even if you just start out walking for 5 minutes a day, it's a start. I will not stop talking about my journey. I am an open book. These autoimmune diseases I am moving through are for a reason. So that I can help people. Even if it resonates with just one person and they begin to heal, my heart is happy.

I am thankful to my friend that connected me with Dr. Lex. She is honestly one of the smartest people I know. I appreciate how much I have learned from her, which has helped me to heal further as well as help other people heal.

CHAPTER 3

THE ENDLESS WISDOM OF THE EMPRESS KAREN

When I decided to write my first book, of course I had to call my best friend BJ's mom. She was like another mom to me. I called her and excitedly told her about a writing course I was taking through the Institute for Integrative Nutrition and some vague ideas of what I was going to write. She had no idea at the time that she was giving me the name of not only my first book, but all of my books in the future. She asked me if I remembered a saying hanging up on her refrigerator when I was 6 or 7-years-old. I couldn't remember what I ate for lunch that day, so no. On a sheet of paper with a black background and white writing, there was a quote that I would read every time I went over there to play. She knew that I didn't understand what it meant at the time, but I had to read it every time. It said: "Life's A Journey, Are You Packed?" Well, I am here to say life sure is a journey!

I shrieked. Karen, that's it! That's the name of my book. And so it began.

My first book was published in 2016. I was so excited to sign Karen's personal copy and hand-deliver it to Connecticut. She has always been my cheerleader and she loved the book. That meant the world to me.

Even when I moved to Virginia Beach, I would go back to Connecticut to visit Karen often. She had Crohn's disease for many years and fought valiantly. I realized each time we visited she was getting sicker. In 2017, I tried to get there every six weeks. We would visit and we would laugh and laugh and laugh as we told each other stories. We would talk about astrology and spirituality. It was all because of her that I was able to tap into this part of my life.

On December 6, 2017, Karen turned 75. All she wanted was her family and loved ones around her to celebrate. She wanted a lovely dinner Saturday night and requested that Chris cook brunch on Sunday. Saturday evening, she held court as only the Empress Karen could. She told stories of her life and her kids, and we were all captivated. She always told us we could be the queens or the princesses, but she was the empress (well of course). On Sunday, she showed up in her furry white robe and enjoyed every bit of the food Chris cooked. We spent the day laughing and visiting. It was obvious she was doing a wonderful acting job because I could see behind her eyes just how sick she was. She would never let anyone know. Karen never wanted anyone to feel sorry for her. As we headed back to Virginia, I knew we'd be back soon.

Karen's disease was progressing fast and furious. BJ kept me updated every day, and on New Year's Eve 2017 she said she wasn't sure how much time she had left. I got up the next morning, packed up, and headed to be by her side.

By the time I arrived, she was bedridden with palliative care. I visited with her as much as I could and did whatever the kids needed me to do. During the week, she opened her eyes and talked to me. I will never ever forget it. She held my hand and said, "Stef, you know how proud I am of you?" Yes, I do. She said, "No, I'm really proud of you and you can do anything you set your mind to." Then, she looked me right in the eye and said, "I love you, I mean I really love you." I really loved her, too. By Saturday, January 6 her breathing had become so labored that we knew it was only a matter of time. It was about three in the afternoon. She opened her eyes and asked me to put the Hallmark Channel on. I found the remote, but it was a different cable system and I had no idea how to find the channel. I handed her the remote. Eyes closed, she put the Hallmark Channel on and smirked. I went to sleep in the room down the hall, and at 4 a.m. on January 7 she took her last breath surrounded by her kids. Karen was a larger-than-life person and she is now the angel watching out for me. The angel that knows I can do anything I put my mind to.

I was able to speak at her funeral, because she asked me to. I wanted the world to know how much I loved and admired her.

No one has ever asked me to speak at their funeral...until Karen did. But that's Karen...she's the orchestrator. Karen was not only my best friend's mom—she was my friend. Karen and I have always had a special bond, a special connection. She was a second mom to me. I always joked that I was the kid she liked, her unbiological one.

In February 2016 something happened and the first person I called was Karen. She and I watched the show, *This Is Us*. There was an episode where one of the characters and his sick father were traveling to Tennessee. The father wanted to take his son to a museum in Memphis that has ducks that walk around. In the next scene, you see the son sitting in his car on the highway stopped as ducks crossed the road, and you realize his dad has died. The next day as I was driving and I had to stop as there were ducks crossing the road, I realized it was the anniversary of my dad's passing. I called her immediately, and we talked for a while. As soon as we hung up, she called right back and said, "Will you speak at my funeral?" I agreed on the conditions that it wouldn't be for another 20 years and that she'd be my angel. I now have the best angel with me.

Karen was larger than life. Her strength and spirit were contagious. All she wanted was for everyone around her to have fun and love life. She fought so hard, never complaining or feeling bad for herself. She was a true matriarch. She loved nothing better than having all the kids, grandkids, and their friends gather around her as she gave her love lectures. With her favorite phrases and words "beyond," "exactly," and her most famous line as she looks at you and points her finger, "Period the end."

As she became weaker, all she wanted was to hear funny stories. Never wanted to talk about herself or her troubles. She just wanted to laugh and continue to educate and guide everyone.

My memories of her go back a long way. As a child, I would go over to the house on Sherwood Lane to play and she would always have my favorite foods. Another way she showed her love. In fact, as the Sisterhood co-president at Beth Jacob, she gave a speech at my Bat Mitzvah and presented me with pickles and bagels. Feeding people is just one way she showed love. I remember having deep conversations with her back then. She taught me about spirituality and strength.

Strength...boy did I need that when BJ was sick. She anointed me as the bouncer. If friends came and were negative...I was to kick them out, as per Karen. My other job was to go shopping with my other girl Jennifer, BJ's sister, to prepare her for her freshman year of college. Wow, this was a big job for me but Karen believed in me. As she did to the very end.

As I became a mom of four, I called her up. Now I'm just like you, I said. She laughed and from that point on our connection grew even stronger. She helped me with everything family.

After my mom passed away, she told me she would be there for me, anything I needed to just call. She made sure to check in with me frequently. Anything I decided to do in my career, she was my biggest cheerleader. She came up with the name for my book, just through a conversation we had.

Since I moved to Virginia Beach, believe it or not, we grew even closer. We would talk several times a week. She wanted nothing more than to come visit us. Since she couldn't, I came to see her. Every few months, Chris would say, "Time to go visit Bubbe." That last month she turned 75, and we came up to celebrate. All she wanted was for Chris to come and cook her breakfast, which he did. It was the little things that made her happy.

I feel very blessed that I had this last week with her. We shared some very special moments, and the things she told me will stay with me forever. Her death will leave a huge hole in all of our hearts. Bubbe, please say hi to Aud and Bob. I love you so much, my special angel. I have two short poems I would like to share.

Do Not Stand at My Grave

Do not stand at my grave and weep:
I am not there. I do not sleep.
I am a thousand winds that blow.
I am the diamond glints on snow.
I am the sunlight on ripened grain.
I am the gentle autumn rain.
When you awaken in the morning's hush
I am the swift uplifting rush
Of quiet birds in circled flight.
I am the soft stars that shine at night.
Do not stand at my grave and cry:
I am not there. I did not die.

Mary Elizabeth Frye

A Silent Tear

Just close your eyes and you will see
All the memories that you have of me
Just sit and relax and you will find
I'm really still there inside your mind

Don't cry for me now I'm gone
For I am in the land of song
There is no pain, there is no fear
So dry away that silent tear

Don't think of me in the dark and cold
For I am here, no longer old
I'm in the place that's filled with love
Known to you all, as "up above"

Author Unknown

CHAPTER 4

DOING THE WRAP AND SQUEEZE

As I limped into Dr. Lex's office on a rainy April afternoon, I was pretty confident she would work her magic. An adjustment or two and I'd be back in the gym on the StairMaster, pushing and pulling sleds, and flipping tires. There was, however, that little voice in the back of my head from my very first visit to her the previous year that said, *You know the rigorous workouts you do at the gym can also cause inflammation. You know how sometimes you only process what you want to hear?* Well, that was me in that instance.

I tried to lay on the examining table as her assistant asked me questions. You see, normally when I go in, the first thing I say is, "You don't have to ask any questions like where I feel pain. I feel great." Well, this time I'm sure she was holding back laughter as it took me several minutes to get up on the table. Go ahead and ask me all the questions. My back was spasming into my glutes and all the way down both legs and I had a shooting pain on my right side. I laid face down and put my face in the cradle as her assistant put a roll pillow under my ankles and strapped these wooden shoes on so Dr. Lex could do her exam.

She came into the room, plugged in the activator gun (the instrument she uses for an adjustment), and said, "So what have you done now? Something at the gym it looks like." It was hard to lift my head, but I did and shot her an ashamed look.

I was in the gym two days prior, even though this pain had started the night before. I had a session with my trainer and I was not one to pay for a session and not use it. So I limped into the gym and said, Hey, not sure what I did to my back, but I think I just need to stretch. So we did. He, and I guess I, also thought it would be a good idea to roll out my psoas muscles by laying on a ball as I rolled back and forth. I rolled my left side and switched the ball to my right. As soon as I began rolling on the right side, I heard a pop. I looked at him and said I think I broke something. He looked at me and said, "You're a wuss, keep going." So I kept going.

As I lay on the table in Dr. Lex's office after her thorough exam, she delivered the news. You have two bulging and compressed discs. She used the activator gun to adjust me and then had me flip over to see about this pain on my right side. She held this silver metal device over my ribs and moved it up and down. It looked like a very thick fork with only two prongs. It was in fact a tuning fork. She looked at me and said, "I'm sending you for an x-ray." I looked at her and asked for what. She thought I had a broken rib.

Off I went to get the x-ray. I had a follow-up appointment the next day to see if my body had held the adjustment and to see if I had any reduction in pain. I was at least able to walk upright, and the pain in my back was so much better. When I walked into her office and sat down, she said, "so we need to talk. You have a broken rib and a fracture in another rib." Then the punch to the stomach. She said, "your days at the gym going all out are over." I looked up from the pad I was going to write directions on what my protocol for a broken rib would be. She said, "With a broken rib and the condition of your back, you can walk and only walk for the next six weeks." Excuse me, did I hear you right, I can walk? She told me I could only walk around the neighborhood, go to the park near my house, the oceanfront anywhere I'd like. So off I went, and I walked and walked and walked and walked. Three weeks later at another appointment,

I wanted to know when I could get back into the gym. Dr. Lex laughed and then agreed to a deal. No gym, but I could do Pilates with Mary. Dr. Lex instructed me to go to Mary because she had 20 years of experience and would give a great workout even with a broken rib. Dr. Lex said, "Oh, and I hope you love Pilates because you are NEVER going back to the gym, at least not to do what you were doing before. Remember our conversation about exercise causing inflammation?" Yes, yes I do.

The following week, I was booked for my first private Pilates session on May 23, 2017. Mary and I hit it off from day one, but I will tell you that Pilates is not easy. It's no joke. All I remember hearing is wrap and squeeze, heels together, toes apart, don't use your legs to push, use your powerhouse (from your ribs to your mid thigh), move away from the shoulder blocks for your 100, shoulders out of your ears, belly button to spine, c-curve, don't forget to breathe, and many other phrases. Pilates has its own language—I thought Hebrew was hard to learn. Dr. Lex was right. Mary gave me an unbelievable workout even with a broken rib. I was dedicated to coming to three classes a week, including one Pilates mat class.

In my very first mat class, there were five of us. There were three black Pilates mats on the floor and two mats on the Cadillacs. I was all the way over to the right on the mat on the floor. After about 15 minutes of work and I'm pretty sure no breathing for me, one of the ladies in the class said, "I just love coming to Pilates. When I leave, my body feels like I just had a massage." I whipped my head around to look at her and thought, *What did she smoke before class? This nice lady has lost her marbles.*

Well, here I am four years later to say she in fact had no hallucinogens in her body and she really did speak the truth. Many days I show up to Pilates tired or my muscles ache or my joints are tight, and 50 minutes later I walk out and when Mary asks how my body feels I say, Like I just had a massage. Then, we both laugh. It is the truth. Pilates stretches and strengthens your body like nothing else. It has been a physical game-changer for me. I've not seen the inside of a gym or flipped another tire.

"You will feel better in ten sessions, look better in twenty sessions, and have a completely new body in thirty sessions."

JOSEPH PILATES

CHAPTER 5

TOGETHER WE GO FAR

In the fall of 2014, Chris and I went into New York City to spend the weekend. Do some shopping, some visiting, and some eating. Well, let's be honest, the first two Chris conceded to so he could do the third, EAT. I love New York. I have a lot of friends there and I lived in Battery Park City overlooking the Hudson River for a year after I graduated from Syracuse University. It only took me a year—well, actually much less but I was in denial—to realize I could not afford to live in the city on the salary of a home fashions trade magazine administrative assistant.

New York is only about a six-and-a-half-hour drive from Virginia Beach to Manhattan, and it was a trip we made a few times a year, as well as on the way to or from Connecticut.

On this trip, before we left the city, I wanted to go to Jennifer's Way Bakery in Chelsea. It was owned by actress Jennifer Esposito, who after years of illness and misdiagnosis was diagnosed with celiac disease. As we walked in, the amazing smells emanated out of the kitchen and wrapped us in a big warm hug. I scurried from one counter to the next having a difficult time deciding what to buy. Should I buy the carrot muffins or the blueberry ones? The oatmeal cookies or the chocolate chip cookies? The cinnamon rolls? The bagels? Yes, definitely the bagels! By this point, I had been on my health journey for over a year and had not been able to walk in anywhere and order whatever I wanted. Oh wait, I said to Chris, Look there is her book! I needed to buy that too. Two shopping bags later, we walked out with just about one or more of everything. I justified that I can't get any of this in Virginia Beach. As I floated out of the bakery with all the excitement that I had treats for the way home and a book to read, Chris pointed at a very small storefront with one bike in it. He laughed and said, "Oh, I bet that gym makes a lot of money." He took a picture of it, and we headed for the car. We looked at the picture quickly, and it said "Peloton" in the bottom right corner of the glass. We tried to pronounce it, and I can now tell you, we were way off.

The first thing I did once we were safely on the highway headed south was open up one of the bakery boxes and take a bite out of everything. Ahhh, it tasted so good and the best thing was I didn't feel achy or sick after I ate anything. The next thing I did was crack open the book *Jennifer's Way*. I read the entire book on the ride home. Mostly with tears streaming down my face as I devoured every detail of her journey. So much of it resonated with me. What I have learned is that it really doesn't matter what autoimmune disease you have, many of the underlying causes and the symptoms are similar. The funny thing (well actually not so funny) about autoimmune is that they like to pile on each other. So if you have one, you most likely have more. Isn't that sweet, they are friendly with each other, just not with you.

About two-and-a-half years later, my dear friend Donna came to visit. Donna is a very talented jewelry designer and has the kindest soul. She came to Virginia Beach to do a jewelry trunk show at a local shop. As we were getting ready to meet another friend and head to dinner, Chris said, "Hey, are you going to be around tomorrow morning at 10:30 a.m.? I am having something delivered and someone needs to be here." I looked at him a little irritated. Um no. Remember Donna is actually here to do a trunk show tomorrow and I'm helping her. "Oh yeah, right," he said. So of course I asked what was being delivered that needed to be signed for. He told me I'd see when I got home. I don't think that's how we play this game, what is it? He said, "Remember when we were in New York a few years ago and I took a picture of what we thought was a gym near the Jennifer's Way Bakery." I did. He said, "Well, it's actually a spin bike called a Peloton and that was their first studio." What the heck does that have to do with a delivery tomorrow? He laughed and said, "Oh, you know, I did some research and I bought a Peloton for us and I got us each a pair of spin shoes." Well, you can return mine, I'm not going to use it. I do Pilates!

Well, the black Peloton with the red and white accents and TV screen indeed was delivered the following day at 10:30 a.m. After a successful jewelry trunk show, Donna and I arrived home. It was on the bottom level of our three-story beach house. I walked by it on the way in and said, Oh, that's nice. That is how I would treat that poor bike for the next six months. I'd look at it, walk by, but never get too close.

On March 4, 2018, I got a wild hair and decided I would try a ride. An Ally Love 20-minute beginner ride. Huffing and puffing my way through the ride I thought, *This is just pure torture.* As I went to unclip and could not get my shoes out I thought, *I'm going to have to sit here until Chris gets home in 8 hours.* As I tried with all my might to unclip, I frantically bent down and took the damn shoes off and just left them clipped into the bike. I cried with tears of exhaustion and relief that I didn't have to sit on that bike all day. Needless to say, when Chris got home I said, I tried the Peloton. Are you happy now? It's a HARD NO for me. Yep, one and done. Chris would talk to me all about the Power Zone challenge and what rides he was going to do and something called an FTP test. All I heard was blah blah blah. I didn't understand what he was talking about, but I did know all about Pilates. I could do a wrap and squeeze like nobody's business, and I knew how to use my powerhouse to strengthen my core, so haha! You can have your FTP test.

A few weeks later, I was thinking. *Hey, Stef, who are you? I am not a quitter, that's who I am!* I also wanted to be able to ride and enjoy this community with Chris. So on April 11, 2018, I took my second 20-minute beginner ride with Christine D'Ercole. I still had to leave my shoes clipped in, but the ride went much better. I'm sure because of my mindset. I looked at this beautiful sleek bike as my friend not my enemy. I challenged myself to ride a minimum of three days a week and I stuck to it. The first few months I continued to ride beginner rides, then started with the advanced beginner rides and finally ventured out and did a 30-minute Country Ride with Matt Wilpers. I enjoyed riding with Matt because he structured all of his rides the same. Warm up with spin ups and then he would walk you through exactly how the ride went. I did get a little confused with Matt Math. He would say, "Okay, so you have 30 more seconds after the next two minutes." Hmmm very interesting technique.

Chris finally talked me into doing a Power Zone Ride. On May 2, 2018, I did my first Power Zone Ride with my boy Matt. You see, Power Zone rides should be started after taking that thing Chris told me about called an FTP Test. Functional Threshold Power Test. No, thank you. Just put in a number and make it an easy one please. So Chris plugged in a number all the while shaming me a bit, but I didn't care. I was just slightly dipping my big toe in the Power Zone waters. I continued alternating Power Zone rides and some fun Country and Rock rides. I finally conceded to take the FTP test as I was getting stronger. On June 19, 2018, I took the 10-minute FTP warm-up ride and then went straight into the 20-minute FTP test. Halfway through, I was sweating buckets, could hardly breathe, and was an instant away from projectile vomiting; otherwise, it was super fun. The good news is that I finished and was on my way to do a Power Zone challenge properly. My first milestone now was to get to my 100th ride. Chris surprised me at the beginning of September with a trip to NYC to ride live in the studio, as he knew I was close to my 100th ride. He signed up to do an outdoor ride with the Peloton Road Riders, and my friend Ginger and I were going to ride live in the studio. I mean, if I made it to 100 rides, I had to do it big, right? On September 22, 2018, I rode a 90-minute Power Zone Endurance Ride with Matt. I was pretty dang proud of myself when I finished, not that I could actually walk. When I went to the front of the studio, there were balloons for my 100th ride that Ginger had picked up on the way for Chris. What a special day and what a special weekend it was. Peloton is more than a bike that goes nowhere. In the best of times or the worst of times, we are there for each other like family. The instructors, the riders, everyone, we are all there for each other. It is truly an amazing community that I am so grateful Chris made us a part of years prior by taking a picture of that tiny studio in Chelsea.

As much as I enjoyed riding the Power Zone Rides, I seemed to get frequent autoimmune flares that would keep me off the bike for several days in a row. My doctor and I decided I needed to back off a bit. So I found rides that were better for me. I cycle through a lot of instructors, but I have to say my go-to instructors are Hannah Corbin, Sam Yo, and Bradley Rose. I can ride with them five to six days a week with very few flares because of how they structure their rides. I really connected with Hannah on one of her rides when she mentioned she had an autoimmune disease and that she decided to turn autoimmune into auto-amazing. Yes, girl. Me too. However, my favorite quote of hers is: "Your body isn't Amazon Prime. It will not show up in two days AND treat your body like it belongs to someone you love."

On July 10, 2021, I rode my 650th ride and I will keep going!!

Don't be afraid to tell your story. You never know how it will help someone else.

CHAPTER 6

LIFE IS SUBJECT TO CHANGE AT A MOMENT'S NOTICE

My friend Heather offered to host a baby shower for my daughter Alana and her fiancé Kyle. We settled on the date January 18, 2019. We picked that weekend because teachers had Monday off, and Alana wanted her cousins from Connecticut to come and my niece Sarah was a teacher.

The shower was so fun. Lots of friends and family from both sides came from near and far. Sarah and her sister Leah arrived on Friday night. I picked them up from the airport around 9 p.m. and they were starving. So before we arrived at our house, we grabbed them some food. When Leah and Sarah saw Alana, all they could say was, "OMG I can't believe you are going to be a mom." We all sat down at our kitchen table, and the girls ate and we snacked. Sarah kept saying, "This is the best food I've ever had", as she usually did. After we ate, I took them to the hotel down the street right on the beach. We would have loved to have them stay at the house, but pet allergies prohibited this. The girls were squealing excitedly in the room with a view. They are beach and water girls. The next day was baby shower day. The shower was such a fun day. We played games, Kyle and Alana opened presents, and we laughed, lots of laughs. Sunday was a chill-out kind of morning. As usual, Chris made us an amazing breakfast, and we played around and of course did some shopping in the afternoon.

We went to my friend's store and spent a long time there, looking at jewelry and purses. When my friend realized Sarah lived in NYC, she said, "My son lives there." She asked her if she had a boyfriend and Sarah said no. My friend connected the two via text. The cutest thing during the weekend was that Sarah would constantly walk up to Alana and rub her belly. She said, "I don't know anyone my age that has had a baby. This is so fascinating. I just love feeling it." The girls were leaving Monday and we already had plans for them to return after the baby was born.

I dropped them both off at the airport, we hugged and kissed, and waved goodbye. About 45 minutes later, Sarah called me to say that the flight was delayed about four hours and that I didn't have to come back. They could hang out. Well, the Norfolk International Airport is certainly not a booming or busy airport. In other words, there is nothing to do there. So I turned my car around immediately. I called Alana and told her to meet us at YNot Pizza in Great Neck. We'd have more family time and grab lunch. Oh, what a fun time we had. As usual, Leah deferred to Sarah to decide what Leah wanted. They're the cutest sister duo. We told more stories of the girls as young kids and tried to solve all the world's problems. A short few hours later, I brought them back to the airport, we hugged and kissed, waved goodbye again, and off they flew to New York.

Sarah and I texted back and forth like we usually did about podcasts we listen to, Bravo TV, and her dates. On Monday, February 11, 2019, I called to check in and wish her a fun trip to Utah. She told me about a few dates she went on and all her plans for her trip. She was flying to Savannah, GA, on Friday, February 15, 2019, to meet Leah, who was living in Hilton Head; she had just moved there the previous week. Then on Saturday morning, they were hopping on a plane to meet my brother Stu in Utah. Per usual, Sarah had everything planned out to the second. She was a bit anxious, but ready and excited to go.

Thursday night, Valentine's Day, I laughed as I watched her

Instagram Stories with all of her besties out for Galentine's Day. What a group of friends. The antics and the fun they were having was so entertaining to watch.

The next morning, February 15, 2019, I got up around 8 a.m. Alana and I were sitting on the couch watching the news. Alana was about five weeks away from her due date, so we were chatting about the baby.

The morning was such a blur, but I believe my brother called me around 8:30am. I answered the phone, and he could hardly speak. All I heard was "...accident...on her way to school... she is gone." What? Gone? I screamed. Who is gone? He said, "Sarah was in an accident on her way to school." The details at this point were sketchy. I thought he said she was in her Mercury Mountaineer and was hit on the way to school. I hung up the phone and called Chris and then my other brother. Ten minutes later, Chris came home and I looked at him. What are you doing here? He came home to hug and support me. I said thanks, but I had a nail appointment in an hour. He just looked at me and said, "You're not getting your nails done. You have to pack, fly to meet your brothers in Savannah, and then continue to Connecticut. I'll drive and meet you there." Kyle came over to be with Alana. He told us that his mom had seen a story about a 27-year-old girl that was hit by a truck in New York City and had a suitcase behind her. What are the chances two girls died the same day? That wasn't Sarah. She was in Harrison, NY, in her car. I felt so bad for Alana because I know how badly she wanted to go to Connecticut, but she couldn't travel at this point. I called Samantha. How do you tell your daughter who lives 500 miles away that her cousin died? We talked and we cried. Sam and Sarah had just texted back and forth and were making plans to meet up and hang out. She and my ex-husband Del were meeting us in Connecticut the next day.

I wandered downstairs to the bedroom. Pack? Pack what? What even happened? I wandered around for 10 minutes and then I had to enlist Chris' help to get me focused even for a few minutes. How long was I going for? What was happening? I was going to wake up from this fucking nightmare and Sarah was going to meet me at the Savannah Airport. Okay, that's what was going to happen. This was all a misunderstanding. Chris drove me to the airport around 12:30 p.m. and then headed on the road to Connecticut. I was in a complete daze, going from crying to confusion to an awful pain of my heart breaking. As I sat in Norfolk, Alana called me and said Kyle said we need to change the middle name of Aspen from Quinn to Sarah. In Judaism, you name after a person that has passed away. I bawled. What a wonderful tribute to a wonderful girl. I landed in Charlotte. I called Chris and the girls to let them know I had arrived. I had two hours between flights. I sat down at the end of a bar, ordered edamame and a club soda with lime. I sat with my earbuds in listening to who knows what. I know people were looking at me as tears just streamed down my face. My phone rang from a number I didn't recognize and thought, *I should answer this.* On the other end of the line was a woman who said, "Is this Stefanie Freeman?" Yes. "Are you Sarah Foster's aunt?" Yes. I then asked who I was speaking to. She said, "This is so-and-so from the *New York Post*. Sarah was hit by a truck crossing the street in New York today. Can you tell me a bit about her?" Ummm, excuse me? She was hit in Harrison, NY, while driving her car. The woman on the other end told me those were not the details that she had. I needed to make a call and call her back. I called my older brother and asked what the heck was going on. Surely there was a mix up. He said, "Stef, that is actually what happened." He wasn't sure where I had heard my story. I thought that is what Stu told me. So my mind flashed to what Diane, Kyle's mom, said. A 27-year-old girl was hit crossing the street in New York City. That, in fact, was my niece Sarah. I called the woman back from the *New York Post* as I said I would and told her that she was correct. At first, I was angry that she was asking me questions so soon after my niece had died. How insensitive. Then I thought, *She's just doing her job.* If she was going to write about her, I wanted info in there from someone who loved her. I gushed about her for 15 minutes. All the while thinking, *Is this for real?* I couldn't bear to even read or look at anything for months. Apparently they used a few quotes. *"Her aunt, Stefanie Foster Freeman, said the young educator was a 'caregiver' in nature and 'an amazing daughter. She was a beautiful person inside and out,' the aunt told* The Post. *'She and I just connected on so many levels.'"*

I wandered aimlessly to my gate. I popped into a salon for a 10-minute back and neck massage, thinking this would take my mind off of this nightmare for a few minutes. No such luck. Sitting at the gate waiting for my flight to Savannah, I flipped through Facebook and a friend of my brother's had posted the original article saying where and how she died. Seeing it in black and white sent shivers up my spine. When I landed in Savannah, I had a few hours before my brothers arrived. As I sat and waited, I posted on Facebook.

> *I really don't know how to say this. I haven't fully processed it myself. My amazing, kind-hearted, beautiful niece Sarah passed away this morning in an accident in New York City. 3 weeks ago she and Leah came to Virginia Beach to spend the weekend. We laughed for days and had so much fun. I will cherish those memories forever. Aud and Bob, please wrap her in your arms tight. Sarah Alexis, I love you with all of my heart, you sweet angel.*

My phone rang as I waited. It was about 10:30 p.m. It was my friend from college, Renee. She said, "Pal, OMG I saw the article in the *New York Post* and had no idea it was your niece Sarah until I saw your Facebook post." Phone calls like this kept coming in over the next few hours, while I was waiting at the airport. Chris had arrived in New York and brought flowers to put at the accident site. They weren't the only ones. Quite a tribute to Sarah was shown through flowers, candles, and notes.

My brothers finally arrived. As I stood at the bottom of the escalator waiting for them to descend, we all just began to cry and hug each other. How could this really be happening? You see these stories on the news, in a sad movie, but in real life? NO, it can't be! We grabbed our rental car and drove to the hotel. None of us slept, obviously, and we met Leah and her grammy at the airport in the morning. Leah and I hugged for what felt like an hour and just cried. My heart broke for so many, but especially Leah. I referred to them as *SarahLeah*. There was no distinction. They were closer than any other siblings I knew. Sarah took care of Leah. Not that Leah needed taking care of, but because that was her. Sarah was a nurturer. She wanted her sister to be happy and would go to any lengths to see that happen.

We all flew up to New York in silence. Leah and I were on the aisle and would hold hands on and off. Chris picked us up at LaGuardia. We drove to Connecticut. The weekend was a blur. We spent Saturday and Sunday planning the memorial service. I had not seen my ex-sister-in-law in years. I just hugged her; no one should have to endure this pain. Everyone navigated the weekend as best we could. Family arrived from out of town. Sarah's friends arrived, and my brother wrote the eulogy. I knew I wanted to speak but could I? I eulogized both my mom and dad. I felt that they gave me strength, and I knew if I chose to speak at Sarah's service she would do the same.

I began to write and decided I did, in fact, need to share from an aunt's perspective the amazingness of Sarah.

There were over 700 people at the memorial service. Sarah was so loved. The family was the last to walk in. Right before we were about to go in, my phone dinged. I went to silence my phone and saw a Facebook message. This is what it read.

> *Hello Stefanie, My name is Christine, I am sitting with my mother in law. She lives in Murray Hill and is a teacher in Yonkers. She was walking to her train on Friday morning, taking the same route she has been taking for years to get to*

work when she came across your beloved Sarah. She is not on social media and wants to share the message below. If you or your family would like to reach her please feel free to respond to me.

"My deepest condolences to the family and loved ones of Sarah Foster. I am a teacher like Sarah and I was on my way to work on Friday, February 15th when I was the first one to come across Sarah. I want to share with you that Sarah seemed at peace and there was a strong positive energy surrounding her. I said my prayers blessing her as I called 911. I want you to know that I made sure that Sarah got the dignity she rightly deserves as I did not leave her side till the authorities arrived. I didn't know Sarah but our paths crossed. I believe in karma and I felt I had to reach out to Sarah's loved ones."

We then all walked into the service, and I eulogized her.

I am at an absolute loss for words. Sarah Alexis Foster was my niece. From the time I held her at only a few days old until the last hug we shared a few weeks ago, she was my girl. We got each other. Even though we were very different. She was neat, organized, and planned every detail, and me? Well ya know I try. Our relationship went from aunt and niece to friends. Chatting about fashion and podcasts, as we talked over each other and laughed.

And honestly you can't really talk about Sarah without talking about Leah. To me it was one word "Sarahandleah." Sarah loved Leah with every ounce of her being. The two of them together was such an entertaining and fun time. Meeting in the city for brunch, maybe a little shopping in Virginia Beach, and just time spent hanging out.

Sarah had a smile and personality that would light up every room she walked into. Whether she knew people for her entire life or just a few minutes, they fell in love with her. I would like to read a text I received yesterday from my friend: "I only met Sarah briefly but did not want to stop talking to her. She was such a gift to meet. I loved when you said you picked the weekend to have the baby shower to have her and her sister there. She loved hearing that."

Stu, I love you. She adored her father. She just told me that anything she or Leah needed he was there, no questions asked. The love between daughter and father always touched my heart. And her friends were also her world. Her childhood friends, college friends, city friends, and teacher friends. I had a few minutes with them last night. Wow, did they love her.

She and Sam just spoke on Sunday and were planning a weekend of fun in the city. Sam was looking forward to hearing her infectious laugh. She always looked up to her. Sarah and Alana shared some special time together and Sarah couldn't wait for the baby to be born. Figuring out when she was coming back to see her.

I really can't wrap my head around this. Sarah, you have made me a better person just by being my niece. I love you with every ounce of my being. I will envelope your Dad and Leah in so much love. I know you are with Nana and Papa. Give them a squeeze for all of us. I love you so much!

Love,
Aunt Stef

So many people spoke beautifully about Sarah. Her friend group was amazing. Girls from her days at Union College and even one from high school. They all remained so close, and many of them lived in New York City together. That was her dream! She had just moved to New York a few months before. These were the girls on her Instagram Stories from Galentine's Day. Her teacher friends spoke so eloquently. Although they hadn't known her long, they were spot on about her.

She may have been tiny, but she sure was mighty. She made an impact on her students, the likes of which teachers who have taught for 30 years never made. There were notes from students that were read, saying how Sarah helped them develop a love for history. That they were excited to come to class and, of course, see her fashion. Everyone in the school always heard her coming with the quick click click click of her shoes or her boisterous laugh. My older brother and sister-in-law opened their house for everyone to hangout, eat, and share stories. Sarah's college friends came over. Several of them had her signature tattooed on them, and the others had her signature put on a necklace.

On Tuesday, we started the trek back to Virginia Beach to return to our lives. Our lives will never be the same. How do we move on? Like I tell my clients, one foot in front of the other. Easier said than done.

We tried as much as we could to be in the moment and celebrate the amazing life that Kyle and Alana were about to bring into this world. About a week before my granddaughter was born, Alana and I were sitting side by side on the couch and she looked at me with tears in her eyes and said, "Mom, I feel like Sarah is holding Aspen in between the space of where she is and entering this world." Oh, honey, I know she is. We hugged and cried.

The following week when Alana went in for her checkup with the gynecologist, they decided to induce her the next day. The following day around 7:30 p.m. Alana got the call that there was a bed available and to head to the hospital. Kyle, Alana, and I headed there. Alana was nervous and excited at the same time as is expected. They got her started with the induction around 9 p.m. Alana's doula Meagan arrived, as well as Chris and Kyle's family. Del and Sam left early the next day and made it way before Aspen arrived. Wednesday evening around 10:00 p.m. Alana got an epidural as they thought she may need a C-section. She was able to relax, and Meagan, Kyle, and I decided to take turns getting some sleep. Everyone else had just left to go home and get some sleep. Kyle and I just got comfortable as Meagan was taking the first shift. Just as I closed my eyes, I heard Alana say to Meagan, "I think I have to push." Meagan said, "I don't think so yet, but let me get the nurse." The nurse walked in and said the same thing but checked her. The nurse popped her head up and said, "We are having a baby!" Aspen Sarah Boettcher arrived on March 21, 2019, at 2:29 a.m. She weighed 6 punds 14 ounces and was 20.25 inches long. Alana was an absolute warrior and Kyle the best support. The beginning of healing our hearts.

CHAPTER 7

TIME TO MOVE

After a few years of living a block from the beach in a gorgeous three-story home with absolutely no yard, we decided to move again. We both wanted a neighborhood, yard, and most importantly a pool! Oh, and a place for the grandkids!

Where should we move? Virginia Beach is huge. It can take an hour to get from one side to the other. Should we look into new construction? Should we buy a smaller home and renovate and add-on to make it what we want? We took a drive out toward the country and saw a brand new development with farm houses that we loved, but it was so far from the area we lived in at the time. Far from Whole Foods, far from Pilates, and far from shopping! So we were on our phones constantly looking for houses on Zillow, realtor.com, Trulia, all the things.

Decision made. Maybe, kind of sort of, we would stay in the same general area of town. We found a great small ranch that had just been renovated with an amazing back yard! We put an offer in and upon inspection there were a few issues. Wetness in the crawl space, the toilets were sealed improperly so water was running down inside the walls, and one of the drawers only opened when the dishwasher was open. Oy vey! We left the inspection with a lot to think about.

I got in my car and drove back over to the new construction neighborhood, Kingston Estates. Chris called me as I was pulling out of the neighborhood, and I started to scream-cry. I'm not buying someone else's problems. Who knows what else we will find, I want new construction! He said, "Calm down, Steffi, it's okay. We will call the girls in the office and meet with them about the new construction." Yay. My mind was at ease, and I knew this was the right decision for us. I can learn to shop in a different area of town, after all.

We signed the contract to build our home and it would be ready in March 2019. We put our house on the market in August, and it sat and sat. When our contract with one realtor was up, we found a Realtor that specializes in expired listings. Within a week, we had a contract signed, and the house was sold.

In January, we went out with our real estate agent and he asked if I had ever thought about becoming a real estate Agent. Chris and I laughed because I had many times. My bestie has been one in Connecticut for over 20 years. I was always looking at houses online and I loved to decorate. I helped a Realtor decorate rental properties a few years prior. We met for breakfast the next week, and he gave me information on a course to take. As I do with most things, I looked it up right away and signed up. Just as I began, the tragedy with my niece happened, so I stepped back. In the summer of 2019, I resumed my studies. I have to say studying for the real estate test was harder than college. I spent hours and days on our back porch studying and memorizing. I passed the course test so then it was time to take the national and state test. The national test was easy, but it took a few times to pass the state test. In November 2019, I was a licensed real estate agent. Just as I was gearing up to sell houses, COVID hit! Then the lockdown.

In May of 2020, Healy came into my life and my holistic health coaching business was keeping me pretty busy. I also realized I really liked real estate, but my PASSION was holistic health and helping people heal. That is what fills me up, excites me, and gets me excited to start each day. Who knows? I may dabble in real estate in the future, but right now we need to make this world a healthier place and I'd like to do my part.

How do you spell love?

PIGLET

You don't spell it, you feel it.

POOH

CHAPTER 8

TIME TO RAISE THE FREQUENCY

2020, a year to remember or forget?

The year 2020 started out amazing. A pool industry trip to Cabo! Sun, sand, and relaxation at a beautiful resort and then a romantic getaway to the hills. Chris and I love to immerse ourselves in the towns we travel to. Cabo could possibly be one of my favorite places of all time. It doesn't hurt that EVERY restaurant is gluten-friendly. It was so easy to go anywhere, from local lunch joints to fancy restaurants and stay on my anti-inflammatory lifestyle.

One evening, Chris took me to Sunset Mona Lisa, a restaurant that has one seating time, 5:30 p.m. for the sunset. We arrived and were seated high up on a cliff overlooking the water. The sunset was breathtaking and the food was delicious. We looked at each other and said what a great way to start the new year.

February was a birthday celebration and beautiful weather. I was shopping for a dress for Kyle and Alana's wedding on October 24, 2020. The lady at the dress shop and I were trying to figure out if I should buy the dress off the rack and have it altered or order one. She said that with the virus in China they may have to close the factories down for a bit. I decided to buy the dress and I would have it altered in the summer. I drove off excited and ready to dig into wedding planning with Alana.

March 13, we hesitantly went to a small dinner party for my friend's 50th birthday. Little did we know it would be our last time out in public for many months and the last time out of the house without a mask. Aspen's first birthday party was scheduled for Saturday, March 21, 2020. Her first birthday fell on a Saturday. How perfect. Well, about a week before, family and friends coming from out of town started to cancel. We were confident up until the last minute that we could still have it. It ended up being immediate family only. Aspen's "Aspen in ONEderland" party was the first casualty to the virus. It was time to start planning birthday number two.

As the realization started to sink in that we were home and in the house to stay, I had to develop a new normal. First up, how to get healthy groceries. I spent hours on the computer placing an order and looking for a pick-up time. Well, waiting a week for delivery just didn't work for me. Many times, Chris would get up, mask in hand, and be at the grocery store when it opened, armed with a long list. He would be in and out in no time. When you eat a lot of fresh fruits and veggies, it requires more trips to the store. I'm not one to compromise on quality; however, I was getting a bit nervous. I learned that I can survive with an off-brand toilet paper and paper towels, but I don't like it. When I was able to get my hands and tush back to my Bounty paper towels and Quilted Northern, it was like a religious experience.

The next order of business was exercise. Thankfully, we had purchased a Peloton bike in 2017 and I was a dedicated rider, but I needed Pilates for stretching and strengthening. My Pilates instructor began Zoom classes, and I committed to doing them two to three days a week. I also added in walking, as much to clear my head as to get exercise. I used my time outside to do a lot of thinking, listen to podcasts, and catch up with friends.

As I was walking loops around my neighborhood, I looked up one day and asked the Universe for some help. I was still struggling with the loss of my niece. As a very spiritual person for many years, I had shut off that part of my life. I sat in synagogue the previous September and just said why? Why? I could make sense of a lot of things that happened in my life, just not this. My mom died young and it sent me on a path to move to Virginia and meet Chris. That I understand. Sarah dying I do not.

One day, I was listening to a podcast I had been listening to for 15 years, the Taylor Streaker Show, full of pop culture and fun, and I heard a guest that piqued my interest. It was Ellie Lee, and she had just launched a podcast called Just Woke Up. It was a podcast with guests about their spiritual journey. I thought, *Hmmmm, okay let me start listening.* It was very thought provoking, and I was once again starting to feel comfortable in a world I knew very well. After a few weeks, on a beautiful May day, I looked up once again. The sky was a gorgeous shade of blue with not a cloud in it, and once again I asked the Universe for some serious help. I need to return to my passion of holistic health coaching. I know in my heart I was given these autoimmune diseases to learn so I can in turn help millions of people. This thought continued to run through my head. I needed a tool to help me do this. Just sitting down with people and explaining an anti-inflammatory diet and lifestyle made people give me this weird look and go, "Huh. So like I have to give up everything I love to eat" and me saying, Not exactly, but yeah kind of. It will be fun, trust me. I have lots of recipes and food hacks for tastes you love. I always get the same answer, "Okay, I'll try but that seems like a lot of work." I honestly felt bad taking money month after month while my clients were struggling. I needed something to come in through, a back way, get them feeling better and then spring the whole lifestyle change on them. Great idea, but no answer yet. How do I manifest this?

On Tuesday, May 5, 2020, I woke up at 7:30 a.m. to a voice message on Voxer from my friend Jenn. She said, "Hey, Stef, I have just come across the most amazing healing device, I've been up all night researching it. Call me ASAP, before coffee before anything. I'm so freaking excited about this." When Jenn beckons, you listen and call her immediately. Jenn and I had been health coaches on this holistic journey together for five years at this point. Wow, could this be what I just asked for a few days earlier? What if it is?

Let me preface our conversation by saying, when you are in the holistic healing realm (or probably any field), people contact you all the time to try to sell all kinds of patches and healing devices. You get weird messages in your inbox on Facebook—you know those kinds. So how do you know what is the real deal? You listen to Jenn. With an engineering background, she does ALL the research.

So like she said, no coffee. I didn't even brush my teeth yet when I popped in my ear phones and called. No pleasantries were exchanged, she just said, "Okay, so listen to this! A friend of mine told me about a frequency healing device called a Healy. I've been researching it all night and it's amazing!" Frequency healing, huh? I mean, I knew that essential oils have a frequency, we have a frequency, our thoughts have a frequency, but that is where my knowledge began and ended. She explained about another device that her parents had that helped them so much and then proceeded to tell me about Healy and all the amazing things it will do for our health and overall well-being. She explained that it had a quantum sensor in it that allowed it to work on a physical, spiritual, and emotional level. She told me it had just launched five days prior in the U.S. Healy is a frequency healing device invented by Marcus Schmieke. He is the inventor of the information field technology and developer of the TimeWaver systems. She said, "I am going to buy one and I want you to be by my side on this journey." She then said, "Okay, so do you trust me?" Let's do this. I went to her house the next day and purchased my first Healy Resonance. That is the day my life upleveled by several notches.

I then did my own deep dive as I not-so-patiently waited for my Healy to arrive. I didn't even have it in my hand and started telling everyone that wanted to listen about this amazing device. I sent a message to my doctor about it just knowing she would say, "Sure, sign me up I need one." Instead, I got a response that said, "Yes, I'm familiar with frequency healing. There are a lot of devices and, in fact, meditation is wonderful for raising your frequency." *Huh,* I thought, *okay well when it arrives I can show her.* Two days later she texted me and said, "You know I've been thinking and when yours arrives I'll come over and take a look at it."

So many people began to start their frequency healing journey with me. The Healy is a Class II medical device cleared by the FDA for arthritis and chronic pain. I was ready to take the healing of my joints even further. About two weeks after I ordered it, (it took a while in the beginning to arrive due to COVID-19), I had an alert on my FedEx app that it was delivered. I literally ran to the mailboxes at the front of the neighborhood. I ran into the house, ripped open the box, put the Healy on the charger, and began to read how to get started. There was so much to learn so I took it one day at a time. The following weekend, my doctor came by and I showed her how to use it. How to run an Aura scan and a Resonance scan. We did it on her, and she looked at me and said "OMG how does the Healy know??" She was very familiar with frequency healing so she really did know, but it was still a bit amazing. She said, "Sign me up." She then ordered a few more devices for her office.

After charging the Healy, I took it out, connected it to the two apps: I call one the pink app and one the blue app. The blue app analyzes in real time with frequency what your body needs. I then switch to the pink app to run the specific program. Healy has become a part of my everyday health journey. I went on Facebook, YouTube, everywhere I could to devour information on this device. I ran frequencies for my immune system, connective tissue, bones and joints, skin anti-aging, and just all the things. After about two weeks of using the Healy and talking to people about the Healy, I came flying through the garage door into the kitchen. Chris was standing across the island, and I actually had started talking before I even entered the house about a mile a minute. All of a sudden he looked at me and said, "OMG Steffi's back, like you're really back."

What I hadn't realized up until this point was that the Healy was helping me heal on an emotional level. It was opening me back up, my soul and my heart. Could this be the sign I was asking for on my walks? I believe it was. I still couldn't make sense of Sarah's death, but I was healing. This purchase I made for arthritis pain was helping me in so many other ways.

In June, I was scheduled to get x-rays on my knees. They had been bothering me for a while. When the doctor read the x-rays, she said, "I can understand why you've been told several times that you need knee replacements." I absolutely do not want that as an option, never have. For me, it just doesn't feel right. Let's use the Healy a bit differently. She instructed me to put the electrode pads in a circle around my knees. Yes, I at this point had two devices. I mean, Chris needed his own. So I used them both at one time on each knee cycling through a few different programs. After six days, the pain was GONE! I mean GONE! A year later and it is still GONE. I still cycle through the programs, just not as often.

That's just my story. In May, I was in my doctor's office running scans for her other patients. I walked into a room to see Dr. Lex's patient Nancy. She looked sad, tired, and dejected. We chatted for a few minutes, and like a lot of people during this time of lockdown, she was feeling very depressed. I explained how the Healy worked and we ran a scan and what came up was Mental Balance. I set her up to run the program for about an hour. As I walked back in to check on her after 20 minutes, she looked at me and said "I feel different. Is that possible? My head feels clearer." I smiled and said yes you absolutely can feel different. I left the room to help other patients, and Dr. Lex checked her before she left and said her eyes looked clearer.

The next day around 1 p.m. my phone rang. I answered it, and the person on the other end in a very upbeat cheery voice said, "Hey, Stef, it's Nancy." I actually took the phone into my left hand and looked at it very perplexed. I thought to myself, *Nancy from yesterday, wow?* I said, "Hi, Nancy, how are you?" She said, "I'm actually really good. I feel very different, so sign me up. I want to buy a Healy." We signed her up, but by this time between COVID and getting the devices to the U.S. from Germany and the popularity of them, it was taking over six weeks to arrive. I didn't want Nancy to lose this feeling. We had a standing date for a Healy session on my back porch, socially distanced of course. Then her Healy arrived. Her story is so incredible. By November, she had reconnected with an old friend from high school, and on New Year's Eve she was engaged! When I called to congratulate her I said, "Guess who needs to be your maid of honor?" She said, "You?" Nope. Healy!

There have been many stories like this over the last year from my personal clients.

HEALY TESTIMONIALS

"I have suffered for years from intense brain fog and intense exhaustion from Lyme and Lupus. The Healy has changed everything. Feeling 'normal' has been the most hopeful and exciting thing I've experienced in my decade of trying to heal."

TERRI M.

"Our family suffered through a traumatic experience that I struggled to recover from. The Healy made it possible for me to get back to work and manage my mind again! I never go anywhere without it!"

KESSY H.

"Three years ago I suffered a traumatic brain injury during a motor vehicle crash. Among my many issues following this accident, I had a problem that none of the physicians I saw could fix or offer a solution for. The problem was that my menstrual cycle had shifted from 28 to 21 days. Nobody wants to have a shorter cycle! I purchased my Healy Resonance 2 years after my injury. After 1 month of use, my cycle lengthened to 25 days and with two months of use it went back to the normal 28 days and has stayed that way ever since (for my past 9 cycles). I scanned myself, vibrated the top program sets and then ran the microcurrent on the top one or two programs. I am not sure which program it was that helped, only that there were no other interventions at this time. When I got the device, my intentions were always focused on improving health and well-being. I suspected improvements with my chronic pain. I never suspected the results I have gotten! I am so grateful for this powerful healing device. Everything is frequency!"

AMY G.

"After an extremely hectic and stressful winter season which included tough decisions like moving my Mom to a nursing care center and forced early retirement for my spouse, I developed stress-induced eczema in my hair and scalp. The itching was driving me crazy. I am a licensed Esthetician with certifications in Health Advisement and a variety of other modalities. Armed with my knowledge about skin and wellness, I was treating my scalp with a bounty of topical holistic agents. But the itching and rough texture continued along with a lot of flaking and dandruff. I was

mortified. I wear black in my job and have never had to deal with white flakes before. I finally remembered to try my Healy. I ran the SKIN program and within 20 minutes, could actually feel the cuticle in my scalp calm down. I was blown away!"

JANET

"There hasn't been a day since I started using Healy that I haven't been surprised by the intelligence of this tiny little device. It has helped me tap into areas of my body that needed healing that I was previously unaware of. Joint pain has decreased, metal clarity has increased and I have an overall sense of awareness of my health as a whole in which Healy is solely responsible for. So grateful."

MARIANNE

"I was originally interested in the Healy to help with chronic pain management for someone in my family. After trying it on EVERYONE in my family. I not only got one, but had to get two so I could send one to college with my daughter. It has helped each one of us in so many ways!! Best purchase ever."

MARCIA

"I recommend the Healy to people for a variety of reasons. Fortunately I am a very healthy person and when I tried the Healy, I noticed I felt even better. How awesome! I want others to also enjoy the benefits. I also recommend the Healy for people to address specific health issues. The device is wonderfully designed to address such a multitude of specific needs. Try it.
The science makes sense. You too will notice a difference."

HEATHER STEWART, PHD

"Healy is the little device I didn't think I needed, but now I can't imagine life without it. It's the missing puzzle piece on my wellness evolution. As a Certified Holistic Health Coach for 10 years, I feel well versed on different healing modalities and have always been in tune with my body. But, as I tell my clients, there's always room for growth. The Healy has helped me achieve stronger mental focus, an elevated connection to my thoughts and clarity of purpose, by supporting my energetic balance, mood and mindset. Proof of really getting your body into a higher vibrational state, which just plain optimizes your life!"

BETH MINCHER CHHC

CHAPTER 9

ALAN AND THE DAY OF ATONEMENT

On September 28, 2020, I was invited to be a guest on Gwen Rich's radio show, The Rich Solution, on iHeartRadio, to talk about inflammation. I was scheduled to call in at 10:55 a.m. and at 10:53 a.m. my results came in from Ancestry.com. I flung open the cover of my iPad to quickly take a look. I set the iPad on the back of the couch and logged in. Chris had just walked in to wish me good luck on the radio interview. As I glanced down at the results, I saw alan2673 Parent/Child. Within an instant, Chris knew what he was looking at, me not so much. I looked at him and said, Wait, Alana isn't on Ancestry? He said, "No she's not, Stef." My daughter Samantha has always called Alana "Alan" because she is her sister and so she can. I then looked in horror at him and said, OMG do you think I have another child that I don't know about? He chuckled and said, "No, Stef, that is not possible." I looked at him and said, alan2673 is my biological father? He said, "It looks that way." What? I then ran into my office and called in to the radio show and talked about inflammation for an hour. Inflammation is second nature to me so I was able to apparently speak coherently on the subject. Chris listened in his car, and confirmed this.

As soon as I was done with the show I started to freak out a bit. How could Bob Foster not be my dad? I mean we were so close! He cried when he and my mom dropped me off at college. My mom had yelled, "Bob get in the car she needs to go inside." There was a time when my mom was going to Florida to visit her best friend Char, Samantha was an infant, and as she left my house for the airport I started blubbering like a baby. The very next day, my dad was in a bad car accident and he would never be the same. He just blacked out for a short time, but the doctors believe that is what kicked in his Parkinson's disease. Several years later, I woke up one morning hysterically crying, wondering if I was PMSing or what. I mean, I was sobbing! A few hours later, my mom called me to tell me that my dad was in an ambulance on the way to the hospital; they suspected a stroke. He had a stroke. We were so connected there is no way we were not biological father and daughter, but, in fact, we were not.

Chris walked in after the interview. He had listened and said, "No one would have ever known you had found out this life-changing information. Are you okay?" I remember saying, Um, yeah, I guess so, I'll be fine. Then he said, "This makes so much sense. You and your siblings are very different."

Of course, the first person I called was my best friend. We have been best friends since we were 3 years old, we know each other so well. In fact, our kids always laugh and say, "You guys are really just the same person." So, shaking, I dialed her number. I said, Hi, B. I have something unbelievable to tell you. Now, BJ and I have been through so much together. Growing up, my autoimmune disease, her brain tumor, weddings, the birth of our kids, divorces and remarriages, the death of my parents, the death of her mother, and we chatted daily to solve the world's problems. She absolutely was not ready for what I was about to tell her. Now, she knew I had done Ancestry and we discussed there was something that just didn't line up on my dad's side of the family.

I said, Hey, B. Bob Foster is not my biological father. I didn't mince words, I just blurted it out. It was the first time I said that to anyone, and it was an outer body experience. She said, "WHAT????? How can that be?" I said, I don't know, but I'll get it figured out. We talked for about 30 minutes. We are so good at talking things through with each other and making the other feel better. At the end of the conversation, she said, "Hmmmm, not sure how I can make this better for you." Then she said in a slightly softer voice, (neither of us have a soft voice) "Well, at least you don't have the genes for Parkinson's!" Yes. At least I no longer had to worry about the genes for Parkinson's, but what do I have the genes for now?

When I hung up the phone, I sat alone on the couch in silence as I tried to process this. My mind went in a million directions. I looked up Alan2673. He was an internist in Connecticut where I grew up. The day I found out, September 28, 2020, was the holiest Jewish Day, Yom Kippur, the day of atonement. Was my mother atoning for her sins? Did she have an affair with this doctor? Was she raped? Were my brothers their biological children and I was the only one with a different dad? My brothers are 10 and seven years older than me so who knows. My parents were the youngest in their families by many years and I was as well. None of their siblings were still alive. I called a few elder relatives on my dad's side, and they had absolutely no idea what I was talking about. My cousin said we have lots of cousins that aren't Fosters, that married in, and we love them just the same. I get what she was saying, but that is completely different than finding out your father is not your biological father and that the whole Foster side is not biologically connected to me. To say the least, it was very jarring. That was the word I used a lot, *jarring.* JARRING: "Incongruous in a striking or shaking way, clashing; causing a physical shock, jolt or vibration." I called my mother's best friend's granddaughter and asked if she could have her grandmother call me. She's 88 and has slight dementia, but I was desperate to talk to someone who may know about this secret. She called me and said, "Hi, dollie. I heard what was going on. Your mom and I shared so many secrets since middle school, but I honestly had no idea about this." For some reason she didn't want anyone to know.

How do I tell my daughters without knowing the whole situation?

What should I say? Hey, guys, just found out Papa isn't my dad and maybe Nana had an affair? What the heck?? They adored my mom and have both admitted that her death was life changing for them. They both referred to her as their best friend. I knew that I needed to tell them even though I didn't know the whole story. They were 26 and 24 at the time and I needed their support. I wanted to walk through this journey with them by my side. To say the least they were very shocked. We spent hours on the phone talking about what-ifs and about family secrets and that sometimes parents keep secrets because they feel it's best for their children. Alana said, "Mom, I've always asked whose nose you had. It's not Nana's or Papa's." Samantha said, "We will figure all of this out, Papa is still your dad." It meant so much to me to have their support. We all laughed and we all cried.

My brother came over for dinner and what registered for him was that we were only half siblings. Pretty jarring to say the least. We were joking and saying, I can't picture Mom and Dad being "together" (come on, you know you all think that about your parents), let alone Mom being with someone else. Holy moly, so many emotions. One side of the family isn't biologically related to you, so now that means you have a whole other side of the family, your siblings are only half, are Mom and Dad their Mom and Dad? I went to bed with many thoughts swirling around my brain. Is this really my life? Has my life turned into a Lifetime movie? How will the story end? I prayed for the happiest of endings.

The next morning was a Tuesday, the day I babysit for Aspen. As I hopped in my car, I thought, *I have one more relative to call.* I wasn't sure she would know anything but thought it was worth giving it a shot. When she answered, we exchanged some pleasantries and I asked, Do you know about any Foster family secrets? "What do you mean?" she said. I blurted out, Bob Foster is not my biological father. Without skipping a beat, she said, "Bob Foster is none of your biological fathers, you were all a product of artificial insemination. Did none of you question that none of you look like him?" Ummmm, excuse me, what did you just say? I think my head spun around on my body. Did we ever question anything? Why would we? My dad was 5'4", my mom 5'3", and I'm 5'2". My brothers were taller but so was my mom's whole side of the family. My mom said that her dad had red hair. I had the most amazing childhood surrounded by both sides of the family and tons of love. I never questioned anything. Okay, wow, I had pulled the car over and sat and digested this information for a bit. Where do I begin to get more answers?

I waited a week. I reached out to a medium in Connecticut. We connected on Monday, October 5, 2020, one week after I received my Ancestry.com results. As I sat on my back porch in the fall sun, staring out into the field across the street, my parents were hesitant to come forward. After about 20 minutes she pulled out a deck of cards to see if that would work. She turned over a Lovers card. She said my parents really loved each other. Within a few minutes, my dad came forward which was unusual. I have spoken to a few mediums before, and whether it was my mom or my aunt that spoke to me, my dad was always in the background. Not so much this time. My dad said his feelings for my mom were so strong and you don't turn away from a love like that. He didn't care what other people thought, it was their life. They met on a blind date and were engaged seven days later. They were married for almost 52 years. He said seeing things from another perspective helps us to embrace the situation. He talked about a secret he had with my mom, that it was no one else's business and what they did was for love. Some things were meant to be kept between husband and wife. He said, "I did what needed to be done, that's all there is to it. It didn't matter what anyone else thought. No one else would understand so no reason to tell." He said it very firmly. My mom then came forward and shook Sherri's hand and said, "Thank you for sticking with this." Sherri could feel her holding her hand. My mom was always wanting to teach and learn. She was concerned that I might think differently about her and didn't want anything to come between us. All of a sudden tears started to flow through Sherri; they were my mom's. As she looked back on her life, she was very satisfied and had no regrets. She didn't feel like she could explain this to me. She hopes that I can forgive her for what she never told me. In that moment as I cried, I forgave her. No hesitation from me at all.

The next morning at 10:30 a.m. I received a text from Sherri. She said, *Hey, Stef, after we hung up some strange things started happening in my house. Lights flickering and noises without an obvious cause. It felt like your parents really weren't finished yet. And this morning your dad was really strong in my ears. He doesn't like some things that he heard you say. Like he raised children that weren't his.* (I may have said that as I was trying to process everything.) *Not proud of that. Just because they used a little biological material from someone else doesn't make him any less your father. You and your brothers are HIS CHILDREN and he doesn't want you to think any other way. HE taught you. HE fed you. HE cared for you. HE loved (still does) you. He doesn't even want you to think of your brothers as halves. You were all raised by the same two parents under one roof. That's the end of it. There was significant energy behind his words. I wouldn't say frightening, but I would say adamant, firm, serious.* We then spoke on the phone, and she had one more message from my dad: "No matter how you were created, you were created for me!"

At noon the very same day, October 5, 2020, hands shaking, I sent an email to my sperm donor dad. One of my brothers found out he had a different sperm donor dad so it was time to reach out to mine. What do I say to a complete stranger at 54 years old? I love my dad so much, I don't want another one. I want to go to sleep and find this was all some crazy Saturday Night Live skit or maybe Ashton Kutcher would jump out and say, "YOU'RE PUNK'D." But nope, this was my new reality. I needed some answers to continue to process and move forward.

Here goes nothing, I thought.

> *Dear Alan,*
>
> *I am Stefanie Foster Freeman. Two cousins reached out to me via 23andMe in 2018 saying they were related to me. I thought it was on my mother's side. After realizing that was not the case, I did some digging into my dad's side of the family and realized I'm not related to any of them. I went ahead and did Ancestry, and you were a match as Parent/Child. I then reached out to a cousin, as my parents have both passed away. My cousin told me that my brothers and I were all conceived through artificial insemination in 1956, 1959, and me in 1966. I am just looking for a few answers that I thought you may have. This is a complete shock to all of us. My oldest brother is only my half sibling, waiting on results about my other brother.*
>
> *I thank you so much for reading this and your time. My hope is that we can connect and chat for a few minutes. I in no way want to interrupt your life. I'm just looking for some answers.*
>
> *Thank you so much,*
> *Stef*

Six long/short hours later I had a response.

> *Dear Stefanie,*
>
> *Good old Ancestry and other. Where could these artificial inseminations have taken place?*
>
> *Alan*

My first thought was he's not going to give me the information that I need. Then I thought, *He put his DNA on Ancestry in 2013, at age 80. It didn't appear that any of his children were on there. Was he looking for me? Was he curious?* I was hoping to get answers.

> *Alan,*
>
> *For some background my brothers were born in Willimantic, CT, and I was born in Norwich, CT, and grew up there. Many of our doctors were in Hartford, CT. I'm not 100% sure it was artificial insemination, that's what my cousin told me. Do you know Audrey Gootman Foster? She was my mom. Bob Foster was my dad.*
>
> *Stef*

A few minutes later, I received what I was waiting for since I first got this news. The truth of what happened. A small part of me thought he may say, "Oh, yes I knew your mother Audrey."

Here is my answer. Not the answer to why. But the answer to how.

> *Dear Stefanie,*
>
> *Here are the facts. I was a medical resident at Hartford Hospital from July 1963 till June 1965 and made two donations during that time to a Dr. Leslie E. Smith Fertility Clinic. I don't know either of the Fosters. What I did was common in those years as resident pay was very low. I was married with a son and was paid $2,900 a year with health insurance as the only benefit. Let me know more.*
>
> *Alan*

Let him know more?? He wanted to hear back from me. Perhaps even talk.

Dear Alan,

Thank you so much for the information. I want to thank you for what you did. I had a wonderful, amazing life with my parents. It seems, you, my biological father, are also a wonderful man.

Would you be willing to share medical history with me? I have had Juvenile Rheumatoid Arthritis since age 3. So I was just wondering if anyone in your family has that or other autoimmune diseases. I would like to talk only if you are willing.

We had a very close-knit family so we are not sure why my parents didn't tell us. Perhaps my mom didn't want us to look at my dad any other way.

Do your children know?

Thank you for corresponding,
Stef

I will call tomorrow in the afternoon. Sorry about the arthritis, but there was none in my family that I know of. My children know now.

Can't wait to talk.

Alan

My response:

That sounds wonderful. Thank you! I look forward to it!!

Wow!! He wanted to talk to me. Seems the two dads I now have are both amazing men. What would I ask him, what would he ask me?

The next day, a week after I was told the news about my dad, I headed over to babysit for Aspen. We played, ran around, and watched the Wiggles. I left about 2:45 p.m. in anticipation of our 3:00 p.m. phone call. I was very nervous, but I have to say as soon as I answered the phone, I felt very at ease. The first thing he said was, "You know, family isn't only biological, it's the family that raised you." I said, Absolutely, I was very familiar with that as I raised my stepsons. We talked about where we lived, his wife and kids, my schooling, his schooling, my parents, and then his wife came on the phone. I thought that was the perfect time to thank them for the gift they gave to my parents and for the gift of my life. His wife chuckled and said after they first did it they would giggle as they walked the streets of Hartford and would think, I wonder if there are any little Alans around here. I found out that that side of the family had a lot of redheads. They were so lovely that when I hung up I thought my parents would have been best friends with them. We agreed that we would like to meet after COVID. I am friends with his wife, my half sister, and many cousins on Facebook. A whole new group of people for me to connect with.

I thought to myself, *If this had to happen, what a beautiful story.* It seems at this point I am the only child. However, you never know what could pop up. Honestly, since I found this out and got my answers, I have only logged back into the Ancestry site one time. Questions were answered and I have moved through this with a newfound love for my parents. How much they wanted to have children and what they did to make their family dreams come true.

I make suggestions, you make decisions.

DENIS MORTON-PELOTON

CHAPTER 10

THE QUANTUM ASCENSION CALL

The Healy is not only about the device, it's about the community of amazing people. Six months into my journey with Healy, Debbie and Hong, two entrepreneurs I met through my Healy team, started a group called Quantum Ascension. The group was formed to help us grow our businesses. Part of growing my business required a lot of personal growth. I knew the time was now to let go of old patterns and old crap to propel me forward. This group is based in Australia, and it took me a while to figure out the time difference. It's interesting talking to people that are in tomorrow! Our weekly calls were on Tuesday evenings at 8:00 p.m. EST and Wednesday at 11:00 a.m. in Australia. I always look forward to them, but truth be told I am much fresher and can concentrate better during the day. Oh well this is the beginning of personal growth I guess. Step out of my comfort zone.

On Tuesday evening, January 12, 2021, the call was called "Love Letters from Heaven," a mediumship demonstration. After a busy day of Healy, Pilates, and watching Aspen I finally sat down at 7:25 p.m. I texted Jenn and asked if she was going to be on the call live. I had tried to reserve my spot on the call on our website and three times it didn't go through. I thought maybe that was a sign to just watch the replay. I took a screenshot of the Zoom information just in case. She responded, "Yes! I want to listen live to see if anyone comes through for me." So then I thought, *Okay I will hop on the Zoom call as well.* So I sat back and shut my eyes for a few minutes and sat straight up and said to

Chris, "What time is it?" He answered, "7:53 p.m." I got up, grabbed my water, went to the bathroom, and got situated at my desk. I only had the lamp on in the otherwise dark room, and I took the pale pink fleece blanket off the guest bed and wrapped it around my legs and got comfy. For some reason, I was under the impression that this was going to be a mediation session to see who comes through to talk to those on the call. Boy, was I wrong.

Debbie led the session. She started out by explaining how tonight would work. She had us all make sure we knew how to use the chat box so we could answer questions. She asked us to close our eyes and ask our relatives on the other side to come for a visit. I sat in my beige padded desk chair, wrapped in my pink blanket, and said, Mom and Dad I would like you to come visit me tonight. I opened my eyes and we began.

Debbie explained that she would be speaking to those on the other side. They will come through her and she would use verbiage that is comfortable and familiar for her, maybe not for us. She did say that earlier that morning the song "Que Sera Sera" by Doris Day kept playing in her head. She made a point to acknowledge it was absolutely the Doris Day version, and it was her mission to figure out why and why that song. My first thought went to my dad.

She began. She said, "I'm with a woman around 87, born in September or October, definitely the end of the year. She's wearing an apron and doing a dance. Not like a can-can dance, but a fun dance." I typed in the chat box that is about the age my mom would be and her birthday was in November. Some other people typed in that might be my grandmother. Debbie said it is definitely a mom, not a grandmother, and invited me to unmute.

I said hello so she could see me and heard my voice. She asked me if I could identify the dancing. I explained that in her later years my girls and their friends would ask her to do funny dances that they would video on their cell phones and of course she'd oblige. Debbie said, "Yes that's exactly it." She was dancing and being quite silly. Very fun, laughter, it's a good memory. She then asked if she was the Doris Day fan, and I said, No that would definitely be my dad. They both were trying to get her attention so she brought them closer. She said, "Your mom was a beautiful woman and in her younger days had dark hair. She was very family oriented and having family around was very important." She then said, "She passed away from an illness in a hospital. There was time to gather around her and all her loved ones were around her." Debbie said, "I feel like you did 24-hour shifts," and my mom made her aware that I stayed with her right through. There was no need for me to go home and sleep. Then, Debbie said my mom told her at some stage someone told her it was okay to go. I replied, Yes that was me. I whispered in her ear that she was an amazing mom and it was time for her to go and be with my dad. She hears that very clearly and me saying that to her gave her a big sigh of relief and a release that she could just drift into the other world. Debbie said she wanted me to know that she's as alive as she always was and takes Debbie on a walk through gardens. In the other world, the beauty of the gardens are a joy for her. Then Debbie says, "Wait, I hear a name like, wait like, okay, it cannot be anything other than that. A name like Audrey." I broke down crying tears of joy. Wow, my mom was talking to me. She says, "It's me, I'm here and I want you to know it's me." Then Debbie says, "I feel like I want to talk to you about a book." I said, yes, I wrote a book and now I'm starting a second book. My mom says, "I want to let you know I'm so interested in it. I'm there while you're writing and sometimes you might shift into this altered space and things just pour through you." Debbie laughs and says, "It's almost as if she wants to claim a little bit of the kudos of what you're writing." My mom said, "I'm here and I'm helping you with that."

Then Debbie said, "Your Dad was a very respectable gentleman.

Very open hearted, a big-hearted man who doesn't have time for fools. Don't have time for rubbish. He has a lot of time for those close to him and important to him. He has memories of the beach and family at the beach. This is an important memory. He wants to let you know how incredibly proud of you he is. He feels like sometimes you wonder. He said you might have gone a different path than what he thought you might do or should do. He is incredibly proud of you." She asked if I had a son and I said, Yes, two stepsons. She said, "One lives far away" and I answered yes. She said, "He said, just know he is looking after that son and the situation and he is on it. Your mom and dad were lovers until the end. There is no separation. They want to let you know they live in a beautiful house right near the water. Everything in their world is as real to them as your world is to you. They have the ability to be there and cross over to here and check in on you, we don't have that ability." She said to take their love and that they are so super proud of me and so super pumped about the book. Like get on with it. Just take their love. I asked if I could ask a question, which was actually a statement. I said that I had just found out something pretty big, that I was a product of artificial insemination. All mediumships say it's not the want of the person asking for them to come forward, it's the need. Debbie said, "Your dad is so proud of you, he just keeps saying that. Even through all of this and your awareness he's super proud of you and how you are traveling through this. But know that he is your dad. He gives me that very clear, I AM YOUR DAD. Always have been. Very proud of you for what you are doing." They are showing Debbie a black and white photo of them. She said I'm going to notice it is crooked and I will have to straighten it again. They will do this to show they are here. Take their love and know that they are here with you today.

This was absolutely the most incredible experience I have ever had. To know that my parents are always with me. That if I need them I can get real quiet and talk to them gives me so much comfort.

CHAPTER 11

HOW ARE YOU FEELING?

One Monday night in April, I got dressed up in my floral Johnny Was navy shirt, my ripped comfy DL 1961 jeans (fitting pretty well post pandemic), and my AGL mauve slides. I was ready to have some fun going to my favorite Middle Eastern restaurant in Virginia Beach. I was meeting a friend to catch up on life and business. We wore our masks in and out, of course. As we sat across the table from each other, we were hopeful about a world opening up as the weather was getting nicer. We are both holistic health practitioners and as always talked about supporting our immune system, vitamins, whole foods, and the Healy. I met with her again the next day to fix her Healy, again masks on.

On Wednesday morning at 10:30 a.m. she called me. When I saw her number, I thought, *Please don't tell me your Healy already is disconnected!* When I answered, she said, "Hey I have some bad news, I just tested positive for COVID." She had no idea where she got it. Was it the restaurant? Wasn't that too soon to contract it? Who knows.

I called and immediately drove to get a rapid test. The results were negative and I felt good so maybe I dodged a bullet. Still not realizing it was probably too quick. I told myself, *If you don't feel good at any point you will get another test.* Chris and I began to quarantine just in case. Me upstairs and him downstairs.

I went home and put my immune support into full swing!! I

already take D, C, zinc, selenium among other supplements, and immune support sprays. As I was running scans on my Healy, programs starting popping up like immune system, cold, allergies, and I listened and ran them. On Thursday evening, I swallowed and boom, there it was, a sore throat. By Friday morning, I had a sore throat, stuffy nose, but no fever. I was so close to 600 rides on the Peloton so I decided to do a 20-minute ride. That gave me energy. Saturday I was feeling about the same so I did my 599th ride, an easy recovery ride. Here is my struggle. I knew I needed to lay low, but I need to move my joints every day so they don't get stiff. Again, after the ride I'm still feeling okay, just a bit tired. As the day progressed, so did the sore throat and stuffy nose. When I woke up on Sunday and opened my eyes, there it was, a HEADACHE. I called and made an appointment to have another COVID test. I pulled into the parking lot 20 minutes early. I was anxious to get the damn test done. I called the walk-in clinic to see if I could come in early, and the receptionist said, "Sure bring in your ID, insurance card, and credit card." As I grabbed my purse, I looked in it and realized my wallet was back home on the couch near my computer where I preregistered online. I turned around and headed home. I told Chris to put my wallet in the garage and I went back home to get it. I made it back in time for my appointment.

I went into the walk-in clinic and handed them my license and insurance card. They handed me a form to fill out with my medical history. It was the usual name, address, phone number, email address, and my medical history. Then I saw it, and my breath caught, father's medical history. For the first time, I realized what I had written down in this section for years was not my father's medical history. Again I will use the word that is the first one that came to mind when I found out about my dad, *jarring*. This is the first time I had to deal with it in "real life." I mean, did it even matter for a damn COVID test? Yes it mattered. It was just another avenue I needed to go through to continue to process reality.

The nurse said "Stef Freeman," and that snapped me out of the moment. "Please come back." She took my temperature and it was 101 degrees. I told her all of my symptoms, sore throat, stuffy nose, headache, and exposure to someone that had tested positive for covid. We were both pretty sure I had it. At that point, I was almost like, okay let's get this over with and let me get it out in the wild. She did the rapid test and told me to go back out into my car and come back in 20 minutes to get my results. I watched the clock, and at exactly 20 minutes, I went back in. The receptionist handed me a folded piece of paper. I slowly opened it up and it was negative! Honestly, I was disappointed. I wasn't feeling well, and I knew after much research that the Emergency Use Authorization shot was not a right fit for me.

I went home and directly upstairs. I laid on the couch all day and night and binge-watched Netflix. I allowed my immune system to fight off the fever itself. When I got up the next morning, I felt really good. Almost like my immune system did a reset. I sat at the couch and stared at the Peloton and thought, *I could do a short ride.* I made a deal with myself that if I still felt good on Tuesday I would do my 600th ride.

By Tuesday evening, I felt awful again. I laid on the couch, ate a little, drank a ton of water, and took my supplements. Finally, by Saturday morning, I started feeling better. You know when you're sick and you question, well maybe I can push myself? Am I really sick? Then all of a sudden, when you feel back to normal, you know, heck yeah, I was sick, now this is what healthy feels like. Shortly after, I took my 600th ride on the Peloton.

I have turned autoimmune into auto amazing.

HANNAH CORBIN-PELOTON

CHAPTER 12

AM I A STORYTELLER?

At the Institute of Integrative Nutrition, we talked a lot about synchronicity. It was described that you could be walking down the street with hundreds of people and lock eyes with one person, not in a romantic way, but in a connection way. I so believe in this, even in the social media realm. Why do we scroll right past certain people, yet stop to read and listen to others? I can explain it in one word: SYNCHRONICITY.

I have been working very hard to grow my social media platform so that I can help more people. Through my life lessons and my studies, I have a lot to offer many people. I just need to get my story out there. I do know that the most successful coaches have coaches. I have been on a quest to find a coach for many years. I thought I found one, but she was not on the same moral platform as I was, so I needed to pivot.

I have been following a woman on Facebook for a few years. I'm honestly not sure how we connected. We had a few friends in common and she was a redhead! So I suppose I befriended her and proceeded to follow her journey. She had a very powerful story that she was able to express in one line: "My father murdered my mother and married my aunt." Wow! Holy moly! I thought I had a powerful story, but this certainly was! I then realized she performed a one-woman show of her story and taught a class in forgiveness. I read every post she wrote. How could I connect with Brenda Adelman, coach and actress, without sounding like a dork?

On January 16, 2021, she posted:

> *Can you share your story – the one that people will stop and want to listen to – in less than 3 sentences? If so, post below.*
>
> *Here's mine:*
>
> *My father shot my mom and married her sister, my aunt. Could you forgive the unforgivable?*
>
> *If you can get that down to under three sentences - you'll get people's attention and get opportunities and be able to use it in your business.*

Wow! This post really spoke to me, so I sent her a Facebook message that said both of my parents have died and I just found out I am a product of artificial insemination. I have some answers and so many more questions. She responded right away and said, "That is quite a story. Let's connect." We planned a call for Monday, January, 18, 2021.

The second after we exchanged pleasantries, it was like we had been lifelong friends. She is from New York and currently lives in San Diego. Her aunt, uncle, son, and cousins live in Chesapeake and Virginia Beach. How crazy is that? She told me that pre-COVID she spent a lot of time in Virginia. I can't wait until travel can happen again so we can meet in person. If this isn't the definition of synchronicity I don't know what is.

I knew she was the coach I'd been looking for for four years. January 26, her *Healing Through Story: Tell Yours! Six Week Workshop* was to begin. I jumped on the chance and signed up. There were five of us in the program. It was an instant connection with these women. So many people have stories buried deep inside that if they can tell will help them heal.

On the first call, we introduced ourselves and told a little about who we are and what we do. Brenda started. She is truly the kindest, most compassionate professional with incredible intuition. I absolutely knew I was in the right place at the right time. It felt like home. The first week we got right down to business. What would our story be? To help us get started, we did a writing exercise. Brenda asked us to put ages on the top of each page in seven-year increments, 0-7, 8-15, etc. On each page she wanted us to put bullet points of what we could remember in that time frame. After we finished, she wanted us to look at each page and come up with a theme. Mine hit me in the gut like a punch, death. Right on that first page my grandmothers died, my aunt was murdered, and my uncles (my mom's brothers) died. Wow, that was eye opening. Makes sense as to why I'm neurotic about the health of everyone around me. I also had an irrational fear that my parents were going to die young since they had me in their mid-to-late-30s. Was this some sort of unsettling intuition about the way I was conceived? Who knows.

Our first homework assignment was just to take this theme and start writing. I wanted to tell my story of finding out about being a product of artificial insemination, how that connected with death. As I sat in front of my computer, I realized it wasn't just about death exactly. I wanted to write about the dichotomy of my amazing relationship with my mom, who had passed away, and this family secret that showed up ten years later. How could we be so close and her not tell me? Does it change anything? I don't think so as I continue to work through this. I will share my piece that I performed on March 6, 2021. My plan is to continue to write my full-length show, to perform and use it for public speaking events. Maybe even a Ted Talk…lofty goals and I'm ready for it all.

EPILOGUE

The journey continues! What will the name of my next book be? *Life's A Journey, (we will fill in the blank).*

As I said in my first book, I do believe there is a place in this world of health for western and eastern medicine. You choose what feels right for you. I do stand firm in my belief that a healthy lifestyle is never a bad thing. Identify what is causing you inflammation and kick it out FOREVER!

Genetics as you can see do not define you. You have the power to change your destination by your journey. Hey, maybe even do a genetic test, you never know what you might find out. My family secrets are certainly part of my story, but they don't define me.

If you have a secret to share, are ready to get started on your journey, or just want to connect, I would love that.

Just remember I am right by your side every step of your journey.

"Winning and losing isn't everything. Sometimes the journey is just as important as the outcome."

ALEX MORGAN

Sending much love, health, and reduced inflammation,
Stef
xoxo

steffreeman.com
stef@steffreeman.com
IG @sosteffreeman
Facebook Stefanie Foster Freeman

MY STORYTELLING SHOWCASE

I wanted to include my drafts and notes from the storytelling workshop that I took with Brenda Adelman, some of which grew to find a place in this book.

MARCH 6, 2021
2010

My mom's infection-ridden body is laying in the big white bed, in the big sterile-white room. I'm sitting next to her, holding her fragile hand. Her life on this earth is slipping away. I'm shaking with tears flowing down my face. I whisper in my mother's ear, It's time for you to go be with Dad. She took her last breath. How will I live without my best friend? She is my mom, my confidant, we share everything. I know she instilled the strength in me to go on, but how is the question. How do I go on? With a shaky hand, I open the window so her soul can soar. She is now living in my heart and soul.

2015

I start having disturbing dreams about my mom. She's always angry with me, either yelling at me or barely speaking to me. Asking where I've been and why I hadn't been by to see her. I would try to talk to her and she would act as if I hardly knew her. So weird.

2020

In 2020, something happened that perhaps explained it all!

Let me go back a second to 2017. I did a 23andMe test to check out my genetics for my health journey. It was interesting to see my genetic matches. A few cousins on my mom's side popped up, no awesome, deep, dark secret story. Two years later, I received a message from a woman Carla asking how we could be related. I messaged back probably from my mom's side and supplied her with all the last names on that side of the family. She asked if the name Hartsky rang a bell. Nope, never heard of it before, I replied and then quite honestly forgot about it. I looked down at my phone one day and saw a Facebook friend request notification. It was from Carla. Oh wow, we both went to the Institute for Integrative Nutrition I noticed. We chatted back and forth and realized we had so much in common, the same smile, the same love of family, and the same short stature. A friendship blossomed. We decided it was time to figure out the family mystery and since these Hartskies that she was talking about all seemed to be on Ancestry.com. In August of 2020, I spit in yet another tube and sent it off.

I was invited to be a guest on the *Rich Solution*, a radio show about empowered health on iHeartRadio as a holistic health coach to talk about inflammation, my favorite topic. No really it is!! I was scheduled to call in at 10:55 a.m., on September 28, 2020. At 10:53 a.m. my results came in from Ancestry.com. I flung open the cover of my iPad to quickly take a look. With my husband Chris standing by my side, I saw alan2673 Parent/Child. I looked at my husband and said, Wait, Alana, my daughter, isn't on Ancestry? You see, my other daughter Samantha has always called her "Alan," because she's the older sister and she can. He replied, "No Alana isn't on Ancestry." As I clutched my heart, I said you don't think I have another child I don't know about do you? He chuckled and said, "No, Stef, you don't. I then looked at him and whispered, Wait, alan2673 is my biological father? Almost like if I didn't say it out loud it couldn't be the truth. I then ran into my office to call in to the radio show and proceeded to talk about inflammation for an hour without skipping a beat.

As soon as the show was over, the events of an hour ago came flooding back in. How could Bob Foster not be my dad? We were so close. He stood on the steps of Day Hall at Syracuse University and cried when my parents dropped me off until my mom said, "Bob, get in the car!" I had two crying fits, once he was in a car accident later that afternoon and the other time he had a stroke. Come on, we are totally connected, this is just a mix up or a cruel joke. (Wait, am I on Candid Camera?)

Chris came back home to make sure I was okay. When I gave him the nod, he laughed and said, "OMG it makes total sense, you are nothing like your siblings." I then called my best friend of 50 plus years and she was speechless. I mean, she is never speechless. She then said, "Well at least you don't have the gene for Parkinson's," which my dad had. I don't really know what else to say. That's very true. Thanks, B, love you. Then I hung up. Now how can I figure this out?

When I looked up who alan2673 was, I figured out he was a doctor in Hartford, CT, near where I grew up. Could be worse, right? A Jewish doctor! September 28 was Yom Kippur, the holiest day on the Jewish calendar. The day of atonement. Did I find out today because my mom was atoning for her sins? Did she have an affair or, worse, was she raped? I frantically called anyone I could think of that may know and everyone gave me the same answer: I have no idea what you are talking about. My mother's best friend Char in Florida said, "Dollie I have no idea. Your mom and I shared all of our secrets but I guess she didn't want anyone to know."

I went to bed and I laid there all night trying to figure this out. I'm 54 now, my dad has been gone for 15 years and my mom 10. How could they not tell me? We were so close.

Tuesday morning I thought of one more family member to call. I called my first cousin, not thinking he would have a clue. When he answered, I went straight for it. Hey, do you know anything about a Foster family secret? He responded, "What do you mean?" Bob Foster is not my biological father. Without skipping a beat he said, "Bob Foster is none of your biological fathers, you were all conceived through artificial insemination. Didn't you ever question that none of you looked like him?" Whaaaat, wait, what did you just say? None of our biological fathers? Not computing. Holy crap. Why was this never shared with us? My mind was blown!!

MAY 15, 2021

She could've, but she couldn't.

VALENTINE'S DAY 2005

I'm staring into my dad's piercing bluish-grey eyes. He is frail and pale, his eyes are speaking to me asking for help as he's gasping for breath. The nurse barges in and says we need to intubate him now. I couldn't contain my tears.

Over the next few days, my mom, my two brothers, and I sit vigil at his bedside. The five of us in the hospital room. We are such a close family. I glance at my mom and I wonder how she will go on without her one true love. He is sedated with an accordion-type tube in his mouth assisting him in breathing. One quick look and I know he will never breathe on his own again. Up and down, up and down his chest went. Parkinson's had worn out his body. As a family, we decide it's time for him to go peacefully. I couldn't bear to see this happen so I whisper in his ear, You were the best dad and I love you. I walk out of his room for the last time, head down, tears streaming down my face.

Here I am back in a hospital room, five years later. This time it's my mom.

Three months ago, she was shopping at Talbots after walking on the treadmill at the gym. Now it was time to say goodbye. When we got to the emergency room three months later, I told them she had an infection in her back, but they wouldn't listen to me. A temperature of 99.1 is a fever for her, she runs 97, I said to the arrogant doctor. Trust me please, I'm her caregiver. They didn't. After weeks of going in and out of the ICU I begged them to do an MRI on her back, after all that's what she came in for. Back pain! They said no! They wanted to do an MRI of her brain. I refused and they relented. MRI results, an infection in her spinal cord that spread to her brain. Shocking, right? Why didn't they listen to me?

So here I sit having to say goodbye to another parent. I whisper in my mom's ear, You were the best mom and now it's time for you to go be with dad. This time it felt right to be in the room; in fact, it seemed to be her choice. She took her last breath. How will I live without my best friend? With a shaky hand, I open the window so her soul can soar. She is now living in my heart and soul. As I slowly turn around, in walks our rabbi. His words of solace: "Stefanie you are now an orphan. You are the next generation." Are you kidding me? That was supposed to make me feel better?

PART 2

MOM HAD A SECRET!

When my mom would get really upset about silly things like UConn basketball tickets and who was using them that evening, she would work herself into a tizzy and say, "You just don't know how hard it is, there are so many secrets." I thought, *How did we get from basketball tickets to family secrets, hmmm?* What secrets, Mom? "Never mind Stef" and she would change the subject. I always thought it was about my aunt that was murdered in 1973, but no, in fact, it was about me and my father. Bob Foster was not my biological father. The man I had said goodbye to 15 years before. The man who cried on the steps of Day Hall at Syracuse University my freshman year until my mom said, "Bob get in the car." The man I had two crying fits over, one when he was in a car accident that afternoon and the other when he had a stroke. Yep, Mom, I can see how keeping this secret was tough. It's even tougher knowing the secret now and not being able to ask questions. Mom you could have told me.

It's been 11 years since my mom's death and I'm only now finding out that I'm the product of artificial insemination. Hello! I'm 55.

All the questions swirled through my brain. Do my brothers and I share a sperm donor dad? Why couldn't my dad father children? Why didn't they tell us? Did my dad even know? Who else knew? Why didn't my mom, my best friend and confidant, tell me? Should I reach out to my sperm donor dad? Does he have other children? Will he talk to me? Does he have any answers? Is he still alive?

A week later, when my brothers got their results back from Ancestry and found out we all have different donor dads, I decided it was time to email alan2673. Here goes nothing.

Hi Alan, I'm your daughter! Surprise!! Haha, just kidding. Here's what I really wrote:

Dear Alan,
It came up on my Ancestry.com that we match as parent/ child. After doing some research (and by research I mean

frantically calling all my relatives) I finally got an answer. My cousin told me that I am a product of artificial insemination. Ring a bell? If so, I would love to chat.

Thank you,
Stef

Six short hours later, the response was "Good old Ancestry, where would this artificial insemination have taken place?"

I responded my guess was Hartford, but I was too young to remember. (Ummm I wasn't even a fetus, how do I know?)

He sent back a response that said, "Here are the facts." Hmmm, the facts? Okay, I'm ready!! "I was a med student at Hartford Hospital from 1963-1965 and gave two sperm donations to the Dr. Leslie E. Smith Fertility Clinic. It was very common for residents to do this as we didn't make much money. Looking forward to hearing more from you."

More from me? I don't know anything. Thank you for the facts!! Now could we talk? I have a few questions. Like, do you have children and do they know? I would love some answers about my autoimmune disease I've had since age 3.

He messaged back and said, "I would love to talk to you. I will call you tomorrow at 3pm and my kids know now."

I spoke with him and his wife and they couldn't have been lovelier. Actually reminded me of my parents. The first thing he said was, "I'm sorry you have Juvenile Rheumatoid Arthritis, there are no autoimmune diseases in our family." He said there was diabetes, I mean, duh, we are Jewish. He also said he and a cousin had a few bouts with colitis. Colitis is considered an autoimmune disease, but who is this holistic health coach to argue with a doctor, one that was my sperm donor no less. They joked that as they walked the streets of Hartford they wondered if there were any little Alans running around.

Okay, so I got my answers from the living, now I need answers from the dead.

As a spiritual person, I had to call in the big guns, a medium, I mean, how else was I going to talk to my parents?

I called a woman I had worked with before, and the only info I gave her was we have a big family secret. My parents did come through, mostly my dad. My dad said, "Stef it doesn't matter how you were conceived, you were conceived for me. What was done was done for love and it was no one elses business." That's my dad, an amazing man. My mom also came to me again in a dream, and this time she wasn't mad, like she had been in other dreams. I asked her why she didn't tell me. "Stef, I wasn't learn-ed enough to explain and it was never the right time." Hey, it was a dream and it made sense to me in the moment.

I processed this and thought I was done. I can accept that my parents had a very good reason for keeping this secret. After chatting with a kinesiologist friend, she told me about a process called Neuro Emotional Technique. It's based on unresolved emotional trauma. Eh, worth a try I guess. Something in me was gnawing at me that I needed to do this.

NET uses muscle testing. As I sat there with my left hand by my side and my right hand straight out, she asked me questions. "Are you angry with your mom?" No, I'm not angry. She gently pushed my arm and down it went. It's almost like a lie detector test, but you don't know you're lying. She then said, "Are you angry because of the artificial insemination?" Guess what happened to my arm? You guessed it. It went down. "Are you angry that she never told you?" Guess what happened to the arm? She tapped on my back with a device to help me release the anger emotion and tested me again, and the arm didn't go down. Let the healing begin!!

So many questions still unanswered. Will I meet my sperm donor dad? How many times can I say sperm donor? Biological dad doesn't feel right to me. Will I meet my half siblings and extended family? Will they like me? Will I like them? Does it matter?

The answers are in the future. Does this change the relationship my mom and I had? Absolutely not! Does this change the relationship my dad and I had? Absolutely not! My parents did what they did for love, which is amazing, but WOW!!

About the Author

STEFANIE FOSTER FREEMAN, HHC, is a storyteller, motivational speaker, Young Living essential oil educator, and advocate for educating people about a frequency healing device, the Healy. Stefanie was diagnosed with Juvenile Rheumatoid Arthritis at a young age. She has struggled her whole life with managing the disease. Stefanie didn't let that stop her from reaching her dreams. She received her bachelor's degree in newspaper journalism from the Newhouse School of Public Communications at Syracuse University. She studied at the Institute for Integrative Nutrition and began her holistic health coaching business in 2016.

Through determination, education, and research, she has healed herself of her autoimmune disease. Stefanie lives and works with her husband Chris in Virginia Beach. She chooses to view her experience through a positive lens and will always take the stairs.

www.ingramcontent.com/pod-product-compliance
Lightning Source LLC
Chambersburg PA
CBHW020913080526
44589CB00011B/579